DRAMA IN THE SIXTIES

by the same author

MID-CENTURY DRAMA

BUCKINGHAM TRAPPED
William Squire in *The Wars of the Roses*

DRAMA IN THE SIXTIES
Form and Interpretation

LAURENCE KITCHIN

FABER AND FABER LIMITED
24 Russell Square London

First published in mcmlxvi
by Faber and Faber Limited
24 Russell Square London WC1
Printed in Great Britain
by Ebenezer Baylis and Son Limited
The Trinity Press, Worcester, and London
All rights reserved

TO MY WIFE, HILARY

We have fed the heart on fantasies,
The heart's made brutal by the fare

W. B. YEATS

Contents

Illustrations

Buckingham trapped, *frontispiece*
Photograph: B.B.C. Television

Pope III, by Francis Bacon, 1951, *facing page* 48
Photograph: Marlborough Fine Arts Ltd

The Brig, *facing page* 64
Photograph: Adam Woolfitt, Mermaid Theatre

Armstrong's Last Goodnight, *facing page* 148
Photograph: Vista

The Lower Depths, *facing page* 148
Photograph: Alexander Low

Buckingham liquidated, *facing page* 156
Photograph: B.B.C. Television

Scofield, *facing page* 164
Photograph: Angus McBean

Olivier, *facing page* 172
Photograph: Angus McBean

Oedipus, by Hilary Tyson, 1964, *facing page* 204
Photograph: Caribbean Press Services

Introduction

Transport and television are the dominant influences on drama in the nineteen-sixties. Many potential playgoers resent the necessary journey and the screen offers alternative entertainment. Nothing less than a world-wide revolution in theatre optics appears to be taking place. Audiences now expect magnified or intensified sound and vision. Actors in the live theatre seem increasingly unreal if they project, remote if they do not. Understandably enough, the effect on enterprising managements has been to stimulate reappraisal of their theatrical resources and they are indulging in a riot of technical experiment, often at the expense of artistic content. In this confusion the obedient script-writer is more in demand than the autonomous dramatist; we may tend to overrate any writer who can leave his mark on a play after the audience-hungry director is through with it. To respect the intentions of dramatists more committed to words than to spectacle is increasingly difficult. No new dramatist of major quality has appeared, and several of the post-1956 English group have been absorbed by the visual media, as I predicted in *Mid-Century Drama*.

In England this period of anxious reappraisal has coincided with the emergence of the first subsidized theatres on a continental pattern. Conscious of prejudice against their very existence and handicapped, unlike Nottingham, by obsolete buildings, the two London centres seem intent on justifying their subsidies by rivalling the commercial theatre on its own terms.

Both shun the image of a Comédie Française and seek to resemble a Théâtre National Populaire, yet neither has shown the confidence in its repertory which enabled the TNP to hold audiences of 3,000 with an unadorned version of Corneille's *Nicomède* in 1965. Instead they have accepted 'ruling ideas' on Shakespeare from an Italian, a Pole and an inter-war French surrealist. In return it can be claimed that the best single production by either company was of Chekhov. It is good to find our theatre integrated with Europe in advance of the rest of the country, provided that a body of dramatic literature second to none does not lose its linguistic identity.

Graham Hough has said that criticism ought to concern itself with 'the facts of creative activity'. One of these facts in the drama of our time is the polarization of dramatic form on spatial extremes, the open and the shut. Another is the drifting away of a term like 'realism' from any precise usage, a trend which has led me to include a section on realism in a decade which inclines more to fantasy. Yet a third fact of present activity is a reluctance to examine the intentions and historical context of older masterpieces, because the moulds they are cast in no longer apply to new work. Finally, interaction of live drama and the visual media takes place without enough thought being given to their different limitations.

This is a book about dramatic form and the principles of production, revealed or restated in terms of current practice. Form, as the envelope of communication, needs to be understood before any meaningful criticism can be made. Production depends on a confluence of the author's assumptions with those of his director. The following studies, planned for the purpose though executed separately or in groups, centre on form and interpretation. It will be found, I think, that even the brief section on domestic drama relates closely to the others. The emphasis on war and violence is not of my choosing but a curious by-product of peace. Not for the first time in history, it is most often heard from those least involved.

For the coherence and continuity of this work I have to thank the BBC Third Programme, which commissioned more than half of it, and *The Listener* where most of four sections appeared in print. Acknowledgments are also due to *The Times Literary Supplement*, *Shakespeare Survey*, *Essays and Studies of the English Association*, *World Theatre*, *The London Magazine*, and for a Sydney Jones Lecture of 1964, the University of Liverpool. I am grateful to Routledge & Kegan Paul Ltd for permission to quote from Eugene Heimler's essay in their anthology *Prison*, edited by G. Mikes; to Jonathan Cape Ltd and Glidrose Publications Ltd for permission to quote from *Goldfinger* by Ian Fleming; and to Jonathan Cape Ltd for permission to quote from *Darkness at Noon* by Arthur Koestler. I am indebted to the librarians of the Institut Français and of the BBC Drama Library, to Christopher Marsden and George Wilkinson of the BBC European Service, to Philip French, and above all, for unremitting support and guidance, to George MacBeth.

L.K.

London: March, 1965

1. AVANT-GARDE

The Theatre of Cruelty

Drama in the nineteen-sixties ranges between two dominant forms, epic and compressionism, *War and Peace* and *The Caretaker*. Whether it is heroic or satirical, epic is mobile and outward-looking, where compressionism is introspective and static. Which form he works in will depend on the way the dramatist is looking at life, and sometimes you will be able to tell which one he has chosen as soon as you enter the theatre. The stage may insist on being part of the show, the way the television studio did in *That Was The Week That Was*, or it may pretend to be a room in an imaginary building. Either way the result is coherent, and the needs of the form have to be met by the dramatist. The epic hero has to be given a meaningful background. Reasons must be found for keeping the compressionist hero caged in. All this involves a certain amount of conscious planning, and it may seem easier to do without a formal discipline and try more direct ways of reaching the public. The easiest of all is to frighten them by a display of physical cruelty.

Here are some recent examples. A priest is put on the rack, then walks slowly away, quivering with the tremor resulting from damage to his motor nerves. An elderly labourer is done to death with a pitchfork; afterwards a severed head rolls into sight. An elderly nobleman, eyes removed by the long spurs of his enemy, is pushed from side to side by a group of servants as he tries to stagger away. A nurse in a mental home has just been strangled by one of the inmates, and her body lies where it fell, boldly in sight during the half-hour before the play starts. Those four examples were all staged by the Royal Shakespeare Company, but they illustrate a tendency to be found all through the arts and entertainment today. What they have in common is a habit of lingering over the cruelty, of spelling it out. Gloucester's ill-treatment by the servants, for instance, is an extra, an inspiration of the director, Peter Brook. Another example of the same tendency is David Mercer's television play, *For Tea on Sunday*. It is an attack on materialism and complacency, represented by two snobbish couples lounging away their Sunday afternoon in a smart London flat. The attack could scarcely be more explicit, for an insane visitor begins hacking the furniture to pieces with an axe. It's the climax of the play. Not only are we not supposed to laugh at the intruder, but we're clearly invited to sympathize with him and approve of his protest, although it's the act of a madman and a childish one at that. Finally, just to underline how pervasive the vogue for cruelty has become, there are two items in the Royal Ballet's repertoire. MacMillan's *The Invitation* centred on rape and Helpmann's *Elektra*, in which the liquidation of Aegisthus and Clytemnestra supplies a pretext for twelve crowded minutes of violence. Last year the Grand Guignol in Paris closed down, and one quite understands why. Its functions have been taken over by institutions of greater artistic repute.

What were those functions? According to *The Oxford Companion to the Theatre*, the Théâtre du Grand Guignol 'catered for an over-sophisticated and decadent taste' and 'specialized in short plays of violence, murder, rape, ghostly apparitions and suicide, all intended to chill and delight the spectator'. If all this has now been taken over by people with claims to artistic merit, then a number of critical problems arise. Obviously the emphasis on cruelty is part of the climate we live in, and nothing is to be gained by recoiling from it in distaste. But the duty of discrimination remains. How far is this or that playwright cashing in on the climate? Is he exploring it; or merely exploiting it? Come to that, which is more thrilling, cruelty implied or cruelty spelt out? Oddly enough, these matters are very rarely considered in today's theatre criticism. And odder still, the climate seems to have affected a number of the people most likely to be immune to it, the critics themselves. You read of dialogue 'razor-sharp', if you may judge by a spate of theorizing in theatrical magazines during the last few years, or 'written with a scalpel'. The imagery of approval tends to be incendiary – 'fiery', 'blazing' and 'corrosive' are okay words – or else it's aggressive, as in 'savage' and 'ferocious'. In such cases the critic has become a faithful transmitter of shocks and it's hardly surprising if playwrights do their best to maintain the supply. The danger they court is a law of diminishing returns. One shock too many can bring on the wrong kind of laughter. At one point in *Wuthering Heights*, for example, Heathcliff throws a dinner knife at Isabella. 'It struck beneath my ear,' she informs us, 'and stopped the sentence I was uttering.' And on the way out, 'I knocked over Hareton, who was hanging a litter of puppies from a chair-back in the doorway'. When that kind of laughter is deliberately aimed for today, we call it sick humour. When the one line too many is left in by a playwright who does not mind whether it gets a laugh or a shudder, then some people call it black comedy, rather generously, I think.

The bible of sick theatre is *Le Théâtre et Son Double*, a collection of manifestos and letters published in 1938. Jean-Louis Barrault has called it, 'far and away the most important thing that has been written about the theatre in the twentieth century'. The author was Antonin Artaud. By 1955 he had been dead for seven years but the American scholar Eric Bentley was writing, 'Today the avant-garde theatre in Paris, in so far as it can be said to exist at all, lives under the sign of Artaud.' Three years after that, in 1958, the book was translated in America as *The Theatre and its Double*, and seized on here by some younger directors. It had an immediate appeal, not only to addicts of the macabre, but to enthusiasts eager to make a new start in the drama and get rid of existing traditions, root and branch. Artaud's attitude to the past was that of Mr Mercer's hero to the furniture, violently dismissive. 'Masterpieces of the past are good for the past,' he writes, 'they are not good for us.' And he goes on to prove that *Oedipus Rex* would not get through to a present-day audience. That is, it looks like proof, until you remember how very well it got through a few years later at the New Theatre, with Olivier, directed by a Frenchman of Artaud's own generation, Michel Saint-Denis. Soon afterwards he makes the even bigger mistake of blaming Shakespeare, instead of Shakespeare's interpreters, for setting up a barrier between the stage and the public.

In addition to masterpieces he wants to suppress the word itself, or at least reduce its importance in the theatre. And here it's easy to sympathize with Artaud, if not to agree with him, provided always that you make allowance for his environment, the Parisian theatre between the wars. Long declamatory speeches in verse were belted across in the French classical repertory and equally long speeches in many of the boulevard successes. It must have reduced itself to a vision of stationary actors declaiming, not too far from the prompter. Nothing in the French repertory calls for the fluid spectacle demanded by our Elizabethans and Artaud never saw a Shakespeare production by Tyrone Guthrie. What he did see were the Balinese dancers at the Colonial Exhibition of 1931. Not surprisingly he fell for them and their language of gesture. They are the subject of by far the best chapter in *The Theatre and its Double* and they are the key to his ideal theatre, which will be a temple of pagan magic, as far as possible in spirit from, let's say, the headquarters of the Comédie Française. The appeal of this to theatre people between the wars can easily be imagined. It was a rousing answer to the frustration bred by commercialism and complacent audiences. To call one's place of work a temple is to raise the status of actors, and there's authority for it in the origins of drama. To aim at putting the audience in a state of trance is the ambition of all actors not of Brecht's persuasion. And so, many theatrical readers have been carried away by *The Theatre and its Double* without noticing that Artaud's solution is typically French and amounts to little more than the advocacy of one tradition against another. It is not nearly so anti-art as it sounds. Under the impassioned tone of the writing and the gusty metaphysics, we're left with this: he wants to substitute romantic ritual for classical ritual.

In spite of his important place in the surrealist movement and his knowledge of acting, bred from experience as far apart as avant-garde groups and commercial films; and in spite of a genius for stagecraft in theory and practice, Artaud's imagination is cluttered with the shopworn clichés of romanticism. To begin with there's the old Noble Savage fallacy, which applies strongly to the idea of taking Balinese ritual as a basis for the drama of urbanized, Western man in the twentieth century. Then there's Artaud's admiration of Hieronymus Bosch, and it has to be the very same subject that obsessed Flaubert when he was at work on *La Tentation de Saint-Antoine*. When Artaud stages literary works from the past, one of them is Shelley's *The Cenci* and another Lewis's Gothic story *The Monk*, both of them exhibits from Mario Praz's chamber of horrors, *The Romantic Agony*. We are dealing with a confirmed romantic, and one, precisely, of the romantic decadence. Artaud roughs out a repertory of nine plays for his ideal theatre. They include a romantic melodrama, the story of Bluebeard, a *Fall of Jerusalem* and, inevitably, a contribution from that novelettish pornographer, the Marquis de Sade. Last, and most significantly, there will be an Elizabethan play without the text, presumably because the splendour of the Elizabethan language is widely held to put a brake on the violence and to control it. So it will be a case, in theory at any rate, of eliminating the poetry and increasing the kicks. All this goes a long way to explain what otherwise would appear eccentric beyond belief, the fact that, out of all possible titles for his ideal theatre, Artaud insisted on calling it the Theatre of Cruelty.

An examination of Artaud's preferences in literature explains the title, but it remains perverse, and readers of the manifesto were quick to take him up on it. He denied having arrived at it from a taste for sadism. The cruelty he had in mind was neither perverse nor vicious, he maintained, but the equivalent of 'life' or 'necessity'. And the effect of these justifications is only to make his use of the word even more sinister, for they resemble the equivocations of the Nazi exterminators. What I find particularly repulsive about Artaud's blueprint for an ideal theatre is the timing of it, within a few months of the first of Hitler's concentration camps. Thought of in its historical context his projected *Fall of Jerusalem* 'with the blood-red colour that trickles from it' loses all glamour, and his wish to replace articulate speech by primitive chanting echoes a political fact. These things have a reference beyond the many legitimate objections that can be made to a starchy metropolitan drama, bogged down in the recitation of classical texts. When Artaud, in the first chapter of *The Theatre and its Double*, relates the drama to, of all things, bubonic plague, his description of the symptoms is lingeringly enthusiastic. The entire chapter reveals a personality, and a personality qualified for the Theatre of Cruelty, the real one, which began with the Nuremberg rallies and ended in Belsen. But Artaud had no part in those macabre seasons, and unless you count it a crime to have anticipated them imaginatively, he was innocent of their excesses. His alibi is unbreakable. From 1937 until 1946, he was insane and in confinement.

It seems to me that appreciation of Artaud should begin with the admission that he was unable to cope with reality and that much of *The Theatre and its Double* is an attempt to off-load his own morbid symptoms on the public. Judging from his specimen repertory, it would seem that his aims were pretty well those of the author of *Sweeney Todd, the Demon Barber of Fleet Street*. His interest for us lies elsewhere, in his personality and his flair for theatrical presentation, not the end but the means. Artaud was one of those men whose effect on his equals and superiors went beyond anything to be accounted for by what he wrote, though there are clues to his charm even in *The Theatre and its Double*, with its screaming, hysterical prose. I can't myself dislike a man who admired the Marx Brothers and could stage an entire act of Claudel as farce. As for the means of production, he approaches them on the very sound principle that the stage is 'above all a space to fill and a place where something happens'. Drama dwindles to a lecture, a pageant or a fireside chat whenever that is forgotten. What he never gets down to examining is the work done by literary dialogue in public. Physical passion, for example, can be demonstrated visually and by music, or it can be packed into a single line of verse: 'C'est Vénus, toute entière a sa proie attachée.' When Racine's Phèdre delivers that line, something is happening. But Artaud's notion of dramatic energy is that of an inspired showman, centred on the manipulation of a hallucinated public. As such it is fascinating, allowing as it does for the use of carnival effigies, musique concrète, and action flowing from a central area all round the room. This is the idiom known as Total Theatre, a necessary corrective to the pedantry which forgets that drama occurs in time and space, and never the same way twice.

It is a corrective, but not a replacement, unless we are to throw out the entire repertory of mature drama from Aeschylus to Chekhov, just because it fails to coincide with one man's perverse, limited and in many ways old-fashioned taste. Why should this mixture of technical experiment and faded Parisian romanticism cut any ice now, in the nineteen-sixties? There are two main reasons, I think, one general and the other peculiar to the drama. Consider Artaud's noble and sinister head in the photographs. From one point of view he's a survival from literary history, an inter-war surrealist, playing variations on themes invented by de Quincey or even Chatterton. From another, he's a prototype of the beatnik. His primitivism, his cult of the oriental, his interest in narcotics, they all fit perfectly, like the dismissal of classical drama as bourgeois conformism, which doesn't prevent him from accepting the status of a contributor to the *Nouvelle Revue Française*, a prosperous magazine of the Establishment. And for a parallel with Beat literature, compare *The Theatre and its Double* with Robert Lowell's description of a trend in American verse, 'huge blood-dripping gobbets of unseasoned experience are dished up for midnight listeners'. The operative word in relation to Artaud is 'unseasoned' which is very much what *Hamlet* would be if you acted what was left of it after the removal of Shakespeare's text. Lastly, there's the prestige of insanity, illustrated by Mercer's television play I mentioned before. This is a legacy from surrealism, applied to a climate of fear surrounding the nuclear bomb. If humanity is organizing its own destruction, then the madman's insight may be as valid as any other.

The present appeal of Artaud's stagecraft, total theatre, is easier to account for. At a time when drama is the poor relation, persecuted by real-estate speculation and competition from other media, the public comes to be seen as elusive and apathetic, not to be kept in their seats by less than an all-out assault on their senses. Anybody who has heard a thirteen-year-old boy remark how quickly the time passed during three hours and more of Brecht's *Galileo*, will know that sensationalism isn't the only answer, but it is the usual answer of show-business on the defensive. Moreover, it now tends to eliminate the dramatist, that awkward barrier in the way of the director's complete control of what goes on. If the ideal theatre is one which rejects master-pieces of the past, then the director is spared a great deal of arduous textual study. Nowadays, with the techniques of film, television and stage machinery to master, he may feel he has enough to do without covering the ground of a literary critic. There is the further consideration that the more eloquent a production is in its language of origin, the less it will be suitable for international tours. Hence the enthusaism for an exportable idiom favouring spectacle and gesture, an idiom which wandering directors could handle anywhere in the world, independent of local knowledge.

What we think of such an idiom will depend on whether we welcome the idea of directors and actors superseding the play-wright. It would probably end in absorption by opera and ballet. But if not, is there any guarantee that a director incapable of coping with an exacting text would do anything worthwhile without one? For the best of Artaud's admirers, his work is a challenging comment on the spatial and optical possibilities of live performance. For others there is always the cruelty and the philistinism, the kicks—melodrama in an avant-garde package. They would probably agree with Mailer's film director in *The Deer Park*, that 'Audiences are made of sentimental necrophiles'.

The Theatre of the Absurd

Although an orthodox avant-garde is something of a contradiction in terms, minority opinion in the nineteen-sixties congealed in the admiration of Beckett, Adamov, Ionesco, Genet and other neo-surrealist writers, indebted in some cases to Artaud. Unlike him they offer a body of abstruse but coherent work, some of it readily adaptable to the popular theatre. How far their egocentric nihilism is relevant to the present needs of the drama remains in doubt, but their hold on the decade has been tightened by *The Theatre of the Absurd*, Mr Martin Esslin's vastly influential book. He tells us about their lives, their work and their artistic aims, and he does it with the exact scholarship and the wide range of reference we expect of him after his distinguished work on Brecht. The whole edifice is underpinned by quotation, footnotes and a bibliography. In fact, an important sector of the drama has been reclaimed from the ill-informed, argumentative atmosphere through which new movements in the theatre have to fight their way to the daylight. If we continue to argue, at least we now know exactly what we are arguing about.

'The dignity of man', Mr Esslin concludes, 'lies in his ability to face reality in all its senselessness, to accept it freely, without fear, without illusions – and to laugh at it.' That is the attitude behind the Theatre of the Absurd, and much of the dramatic technique follows logically from it. If reality is meaningless, a circular progress by man from nothing to nothing in a universe with no God, then the classical forms of dramatic construction no longer apply. Action rising through complications to a climax can be discarded. So can character, a convention at variance with the facts of being. So can plot. Along with Aristotelian construction, out goes the epic, because you can't have an epic hero dedicated to nothing. And whenever possible, we get rid of language, too. For, as is well known, language is a barrier to communication. It is exploited by politicians, it is murdered by the uneducated and the bourgeoisie has frozen it into an exchange of clichés.

Having denied itself all these weapons of traditional drama, what does the Theatre of the Absurd make use of instead? Social realism, perhaps? Definitely not. Apart from its affiliations with political propaganda, realism tends to look on the conflicts of humanity from outside, whereas – so the argument runs – the true field of battle is inside us, in the Unconscious. The Theatre of the Absurd attacks us below the threshold of consciousness, mainly by visual devices and by language in a state of fragmentation, in short, by a kind of intellectual clowning. Ionesco, for example, excels in contrasting the two methods. There will be the legs of a giant corpse on the stage, and the owners of the room will be talking in a parody of ordinary conversation. The horror is too big for them. Their humanity, in the circumstances, is inadequate, ridiculous.

Mr Esslin claims that the effect on us is therapeutic, that it conveys to us the reality of the human condition. How far we agree with him will depend on two things: our feelings in the theatre and our estimate of the view of life these authors put forward. As a drama critic, I often have to separate the surface impact of a play from my final estimate of it, because what is immediately exciting or disturbing doesn't always turn out in the end to have been significant. In Ionesco, and sometimes in Beckett, there's a theatrical exhibitionism, typical of avant-garde intellectuals who think they are doing the theatre a favour by having anything to do with it at all. Ionesco had a lot of fun demolishing the conventions of bouleward theatre, an easy target. Then he tried acting himself, and his comments on the experience could hardly be more obvious or conventional. Any amateur actor could tell you as much. I think this dilettante attitude endangers the entire movement. Beckett's *Endgame*, for example, disregards the limitations of a living audience. It has one fatal defect – monotony.

Now in Strindberg, you don't find this playfulness and condescension. At his most adventurous, he is too passionately concerned with what he is expressing to enjoy himself with formal experiments. The experiments are there, but they are digested in the play like the mummy in *The Ghost Sonata*. And he never appears to fall in love with his own dialogue in the way Ionesco and Beckett often do. Their dialogue can be so witty and artificial in a literary way, that it creates a pedantic atmosphere, more suited to a classroom than a theatre. No wonder they are so anxious to reinforce it by gimmicks borrowed from expressionism, surrealism, burlesque and the cinema.

At its best, in *Waiting for Godot* or *The Chairs*, the Theatre of the Absurd does make an original idiom out of all this. It has something like the quality of a string quartet, in comparison with the broader, symphonic handling of similar themes by Racine, Shakespeare and the Greeks. As such, although Mr Esslin would disagree with me, I think its appeal is to a minority and I don't think its connection with the comic art of Chaplin, the Marx Brothers and Tati goes deep. The work of these great comedians never plays with horror. It's basically humane and benevolent; unlike the fashionable 'sick humour', which depends like the Theatre of the Absurd, on an inhuman response.

The main concern of the Theatre of the Absurd is with mankind in despair, with the doomed individual, alone in Pascal's illimitable spaces and bitterly joking. Now that's a heroic task for the playwright. How well are Ionesco, Beckett and Genet equipped for it? As men they lived through the reality of enemy occupation during the Second World War, an ordeal we in Britain were spared. They draw their heroic pessimism from that experience, I think, and lacking it, their imitators in other countries seem only frivolous and pretentious.

What I am not happy about is the ancestry which Mr Esslin traces for the Theatre of the Absurd from the decadence of the

Romantic Movement. If lack of communication between human beings is a major problem in the nineteen-sixties, then the cult of perversity and eccentricity seems an unlikely way of arriving at a solution. One of the dangers of communicating below the level of consciousness is to let loose primitive forces beyond the control of the playwright. It happens every time a film intending to condemn concentration camps gives the audience a sadistic thrill. What is there to prevent the result from being infective rather than therapeutic? Artaud's primitivism, in particular, does have links with the life-loving sources of Henry Moore and Picasso. But his notion of drama dehumanizes it in three different ways: by an ambiguous attitude to cruelty, by contempt for language and by a break with the literary wisdom of the past. In so far as it conforms to that doctrine, the Theatre of the Absurd may turn out to have been a brilliant aberration, without much of a future.

The Lion Tamers

In films of twenty and thirty years ago an angry lover would hurl a cup of coffee in his girl friend's face, or a hoodlum knock the victim cold and then grind his fallen spectacles briskly to fragments on the office carpet. Compared with that, there is something effete and spurious about today's avant-garde cult of violence in the arts, not least in drama. All the same, it does partly represent an attempt to harness intractable impulses. I think our power to control violence, as well as to discuss its artistic use, would be greater, if we could start with a workable definition.

In everyday life there's little or no confusion about defining it. By and large it is behaviour directed against the person. It is illegal. It gets you into trouble from the referee of a football match or, worse, the police. And it is objective; letting loose ugly thoughts alone in the ivory tower doesn't count. How the criminal law regards it is illustrated by two cases from the American South. In one of them a Negro cleaner rested his hands for a second or two on the shoulders of a white woman alone in a library, and told her she had worked long enough. Allowing for segregation, the context in fact, even this minimum violence amounted to an assault. The offender seems to have thought so, anyway. He fled. The other case centred on a woman who panicked when she heard a car engine cut out on her way through the woods. A few minutes before the driver had stopped near her farm, 'leering at me', as she described it, 'a curious look'. This counts as less than action, and he was acquitted. To constitute an assault, say the American experts who cite the two cases, 'there must be an overt act or an attempt, or the unequivocal appearance of an attempt, with force and violence, to do some immediate physical injury to the person of another'. Adopt this definition, regard evidence, as in everyday life we do, as a matter for the criminal law, consider works of art from this point of view, and at least we have a clear starting place.

The Institute of Contemporary Art's exhibition in 1964 of Violence in Society, Nature and Art, divided its subject-matter into five categories. Four of these categories, Protests, Creation of New Forms, Direct Expression of Violence and Symbolic Violence, would be eliminated by this definition. In none of them, from the legal aspect, is the artist doing any more than leering a curious look. He can lash on the paint in a white fury, ride a scooter over the canvas, razor it into ribbons or project wicked dreams. Society couldn't care less, because none of these are offences against a person. Neither are the representations in the remaining category, but they mostly come to grips with situations which the law would take notice of if the things represented were facts. The artist in any medium is then using subject-matter parallel with human actions, their causes and results. Where the exhibition's programme advocates broadening the image of violence, I am in favour of narrowing it.

Often the axis of great art on the stage, in painting or the novel, is criminal assault of one kind or another. The problem solved in *Hamlet* is how to have a king killed in an acceptable way. Before bringing it off, Hamlet murders Polonius and loses the tactical initiative from that moment. The Thebans and Atrides in Greek tragedy are interesting first and foremost as killers. Battle painters may stress perspective, like Uccello, or contorted bodies like Michelangelo, but their theme is killing. The crucial act of violence can occur at the end, as in *Hamlet*, with everything else as the lead-in; or at the very beginning, as in *Crime and Punishment*, with everything else as the consequence. What all these artists have in common is our agreement that their violence is significant. They have digested it into a body of myth, poetry, philosophy or formal structure. They break even in the unresolved struggle between man and the beast in himself. In terms of an artifact they may be said to have won the struggle, but it must be a dangerous and exhausting business even on the plane of fiction. Like lion taming it needs a special kind of personality and a tough constitution, as well as technique. When these are present, we feel a tremendous tension between artist and subject –not only the tension between Hemingway's matador and his bull, but the tension between Hemingway and both of them. Or, for that matter, the tension between Shakespeare and an act of violence at the moment of the putting out of Gloucester's eyes. There, Shakespeare is risking an act of gross realism, contrary to all accepted theory of serious drama, in the hope that he has already done enough in *King Lear* to keep the main action going around and through it. Whether he succeeds or not is an open question, but he is hoping that this horror can be digested in the context. If not, the assault, by tragic standards, is insignificant.

'*See* better, Lear' says Kent, stating a recurrent theme, and there is logic in the loss of Gloucester's eyes. The incident isn't gratuitous. Violence never is, I think, in really good work, unless we regroup our ideas around Gide's hero who pushed a complete stranger out of a train. In any case, Gide's novel explains why Lafcadio's seemingly gratuitous action is in character, and by that much the less gratuitous. Similarly, if Sartre's play about Resistance workers being tortured is anything more than melodrama, it's because of the intellectual context, the tension of ideas. This is particularly true of the *Les Mains sales*, where most of the action leads up to a political assassination which one is liable to remember as a drastic twist in the argument. The middle and late plays of Brecht have violent incidents, deeply embedded in a master plan, like the murder of a coolie by a merchant in *The Exception and the Rule*. Here the violence resolves a significant relationship and precipitates involved, ironical discussion at the merchant's trial. In all these examples violence remains an incident, no matter how crucial, in a chain of causes and consequences. The tendency is to *place* violence, not just accept it or exploit it for frightening the public. One is aware throughout of the intervention of a mind, of a controlling process like the legal machinery which acquitted the man I mentioned earlier, the motorist who gave the woman a curious look. The great artists always bring their minds as well as their nerves to bear on violence. The others are too excitable, too easily infected, too much concerned with symptoms. A jury composed of them would have decided that case by looking no further than the woman's panic.

I think the excitable climate we live in now, and from which the arts often take their tone, is a product of recent history, notably the concentration camps, of cruelty as a systematic instrument of policy. England only got wind of it in the thirties. An incident in one of Graham Greene's entertainments brings out vividly its impact on the insular security existing before. A foreign agent, late for a rendezvous with a girl in Piccadilly Circus, explains that he has just been shot at. She's convinced that such things don't happen here–until he points to the bullet marks on the wall of the Prudential Assurance building. He has brought the incredible future, the new Europe, with him–as Malraux and Hemingway were to bring it indirectly, by their novels, from the Spanish Civil War. From Malraux and Hemingway I think we can lay down the principle that our century's violence is better left to writers with direct combat experience. Previously this was not necessary, because, perhaps, everyone was accustomed to witnessing a certain amount of personal violence in the streets. Nowadays, however, the fantasies of any artist looking at these things from a sheltered life soon wear thin. Too much has been done by others, with real authority. Here, for example, is Malraux describing a political murder in the Far East: 'One move and the man would have ceased to live. To kill him was nothing; it was touching him that was impossible. And the blow had to be delivered with the utmost precision. The sleeper, lying on his back in his European style of bed, wore only a short pair of pants; but his ribs were invisible under the loose flesh. Chen would have to take aim from the position of the man's nipples. He knew how difficult it is to strike directly downwards. He held the blade of his dagger up in the air, but the left breast was the farther from him, with the mesh of the mosquito-net in the way he would have to strike at arm's length–following a curve, like the swing in boxing. He altered the angle of the dagger, so that now the blade was horizontal. To touch this motionless body was as difficult as touching a corpse; possibly for the same reasons.'

Writing like that, of course, is a product of creative imagination, literary merit. But the artistic handling of violence is responsible. It is controlled by first-hand observation, just as violence in tragedy was controlled by the classical rules or by verse. Without the experience, you get the fantasies of a writer like the Royal Shakespeare's current idol, Antonin Artaud – neurotic, late Romantic, sensationalist. After prolonged exposure to it as a theatre critic, a film critic, a reader, a television viewer and a devotee of painting, I find this kind of souped-up, subjective, amateur's violence, a massive bore. Coming, as it so often does, from people with no first-hand experience of war, medical work or even competitive sport, how could it be anything else? But some attempt can be made to isolate the factors leading to the vogue, and there seem to be three obvious places to look for them: recent history, the prevailing social climate, and vested interests.

The dominant historical event, of course, is the Second World War, a good deal of which can still be interpreted as 'legal' violence, sanctioned by ideas and a cause and digested into pre-nuclear, pre-Belsen military tradition. Although, for example, I have seen battle-shocked survivors of the Anzio landings lurching around under the orange trees of a backward area, allegedly convalescent, I've also known survivors of a bitterly opposed landing in Sicily who described it as 'cushy'. To them it was, because they were veteran killers in the context of an efficient machine, the Eighth Army. In that spirit I can now read the history of these campaigns with detachment, as an intellectual exercise, the horrors removed by a kind of alienation technique. If I could do the same for Auschwitz and Belsen, there would be something seriously wrong with me. There, for the first time on such a scale, violence lost all sanctions and became, systematically, not an aberration, but the norm. The human imagination had not fully evolved the means to cope with it, and the kindest thing one can say about indiscriminate violence in the arts, is that it partly represents an attempt to find them. The arts are trying to get their bearings after a revolution in human conduct. Naturally, most of the attempts are failures and merely give the dynamic of cruelty a wider circulation. When the failure is that of a hyper-sensitive, hysterical nature like Artaud's, it's possible to fear that only a slight change in the field of interest could turn the artist into a concentration camp guard. In art of his sort, there's no intervention of a mind between us and the subject-matter, because the mind itself is legally 'unsound', disintegrated. There's no tension between the lion-tamer and the beast. He's abdicated and let it loose in the Big Top. It's a mangy beast, anyway, with little of the power conferred by draughtsmanship and anatomy on the lion painted by Stubbs. But it's vicious enough.

It used to be thought that Hitler's secret weapon was a ballistic missile, the V2 rocket, but a more insidious weapon turns out to have been the camps. More than thirty years after, the facts about them are still being disseminated in films, television and paper-backs, to a younger generation with little direct experience of violence. There is a vacuum which used to be filled, deplorably enough, by the facts and mystique of conventional war. And into this vacuum are steadily pumped the indigestible, inconceivable facts of Auschwitz and Belsen, the first societies in which assault became a monotonous routine, no longer criminal. When the flow of information slackens, trials of recently discovered offenders act as a booster. The circle of contamination widens. All this is preferable to suppressing the facts, but it exposes society to a very painful process of assimilation, and facile violence in the arts is one of the side effects. In addition to the new in-exhaustible source in history, new means of diffusion have grown up. Television gives the flow of guilt and horror an unheard-of availability. The cinema, slowly getting free from an embargo on sex, behaves like a voyeur of insolence, patiently obsessed. The theatre lets its hair down in nihilistic surrealist pieces derived from France under Nazi occupation or points up the butchery in the Wars of the Roses. It's difficult to distinguish where the arts reflect a savage, jittery climate and where they contribute to it, and much the same can be said of psychiatry, which creates as many problems as it solves, because of its misuse by third-rate fiction writers. We've all grown proud of possessing an only partially domesticated animal of our own, our Id. And it may well be that the more streamlined and secure life is, the more we spoil it and envy its claws and teeth. The latest trend in domestic drama is a vicious take-over of the home itself.

'Anthropologists will demonstrate,' say the notes on the ICA exhibition, 'that both sane and insane expressions of violence are culturally determined.' Well, I don't know whether that includes the availability of the fictional product *violence* but I suppose it might. Perhaps, it's worth taking a glance at the state of the market from the point of view of an addict with a day's leisure to get through in London. At breakfast, if his luck's really in, he can read newspaper reports of surgical experiments on non-consenting minors and adults in the Dering libel case. On his way to a mid-morning horror film he can buy what he needs from a wide selection of paperbacks ranging from Mickey Spillane to the historical facts of atrocity. In the lunch hour on his way to the afternoon showing of a sadistic film epic, there will be time to take in an art exhibition with an odds-on chance of finding Goya's influence somewhere, or at least Francis Bacon's. After the film there will be a dreary interlude for dinner, enlivened a little by evening newspaper reports of this day's continuation of the Dering Case. Then comes the full range of choice. Two more films, perhaps, but not necessarily. There's a long-running stage success from a novel by an Oxford philosophy don. It has a samurai sword in it and it's called *A Severed Head*. At the Aldwych, it may be a night for *Edward IV* – whoever wrote that:

> *Off with the crown, and with the crown, his head*
> *And, whilst we breathe, take time to do him dead.*

York has his face rubbed with a napkin steeped in his son's blood, all culturally determined by the original text, set down – with a few exceptions – in choice Tudorese, often unintentionally funny. In the higher reaches of the theatre, severed heads are becoming obligatory. Our addict may have enjoyed seeing one in Euripides's *The Bacchae*. For the evening's intake, of course, he may decide to rely on television, reading torture memoirs during the natural breaks. Although this man's consumption of fictional violence is gluttonous, it's merely an exaggeration of our normal diet. His environment favours excess, because so many people have a vested interest in keeping up the supply. It may be true that the pop art violence of Victorian melodrama and screen epics does people good, but surely not in such quantity, so continuously and by such powerful means of diffusion? And with Auschwitz just round the corner. Nobody claims that the Romans had any kind of catharsis from the Coliseum. The assumption behind much of the violence in popular fiction is that 'life is cheap'. It's an ignorant, infantile assumption, but a transferable one. Witness sick humour, or the way old-age pensioners are expected to match their eyesight and reflexes against fast cars on any road.

In this climate, under pressure from middlemen and the public, the tendency of all the arts has been towards the short cut, violence for the kicks, towards immersion in the subject-matter rather than control of it. For example, there was a case of a man who killed his child during sleep, thinking he was struggling with a wild tiger. Relate the bare facts in a sentence and the result is sick humour. Approach them with the measured intelligence of the criminal law, and you enter the climate of serious art. With Brechtian poise and irony an expert records the verdict: '(He) was not convicted of murder, nor, indeed, of anything.' The artist who deals in violence faces the beast alone. Experience and the tools of his craft are his only means of investigation. He needs strong nerves and the soundest of minds, and his search may not lead him, as is often supposed, in the direction of a classical decorum and detachment foreign to the climate of our time. It may lead him, and us with him, into greater violence on the way to his solution, into waters where the hack writer's fantasies would not make a ripple. The hero of the novel by Malraux which I've already quoted, dies from cyanide, gratefully self-administered in his situation. His deliverer, the owner of the capsule, is executed by being thrust into the furnace of a loco-motive. One of the survivors debates an old proverb to the effect that it takes nine months to make a man and a day to destroy him. It doesn't, he thinks, take nine months to make a man. It takes fifty years. Either way, life is not cheap.

2. COMPRESSIONISM

The Form

Francis Bacon is a painter celebrated for his rendering of enclosure and terror. In the series of variations on Velázquez's portrait of Pope Innocent X, the cardinal is caged in a rectangle within the outer rectangle formed by the picture's frame. He is trapped, and his mouth is disfigured by the expressionist painter's equivalent of a scream. In other paintings by Bacon, the formula recurs, only the victim is no longer a prelate. He wears the lounge suit which is equally the uniform of a present-day tycoon or politician. But he too is in a trap, screaming. In front of these paintings we are grimly at home. There's no need to spell out the message. Not the least horrifying part of it is that we recognize it instantly as one of the commonplaces of our time. It is not the message of one painter's tortured personality, but fair comment on the new barbarism, also made by what are sometimes thought of as irreconcilable opposites, that is, philosopher and clown. One of Marcel Marceau's best known mime pieces is called *La Cage*. He begins like an animal, fingering the bars of his prison one after the other. At length he gets out, straightens up and becomes human. The piece ends when he finds that outside the first cage is another one, another set of bars. The philosopher is equally explicit. In *La Chute*, Albert Camus's narrator recalls an internment camp near Tripoli. 'I'll not describe it to you,' he says. 'We children of this half-century don't need a diagram to imagine such places. A hundred and fifty years ago, people became sentimental about lakes and forests. Today we have the lyricism of the prison cell.'

The sources of this attitude in recent history are evident enough. As for the arts, they would be hopelessly out of touch if they failed to reflect it. In the case of drama, however, the cage and the scream have been reflected by a new form which has taken shape over the last sixty years or so. For some time the formal categories of tragedy, comedy and so forth, have borne little relation to the actual course of dramatic writing, and various new labels – dark comedy, theatre of cruelty and so on – have been in circulation. If any of these new labels is to stick, it's necessary that it should bear a close relationship to what is actually happening in the drama, and that it should be a help, rather than a hindrance, to critical discussion. On such grounds, for example, one may object to 'dark comedy' as a term applicable to both Shakespeare and Pinter. Apart from anything else, the two historical backgrounds involved are too divergent for any joint label to carry conviction. Therefore, the onus on anybody putting forward, as I am now, a new name for a formal category not previously isolated, is particularly heavy. I think it can be sustained in the case of Compressionism, a principle which unites the allusions to Bacon, Marceau and Camus already made. To begin with a provisional definition: 'A compressionist play is one in which the characters are insulated from society in such a way as to encourage the maximum conflict of attitudes.'

As we trace the history of the form, we shall notice that the degree of insulation varies, that the attitudes in collision can be intellectual and/or emotional, and so on. There will be the usual risks of a false inclusiveness, such as lumping *Huis-Clos* and *Man and Superman* together, because they both deal with people in Hell. Fortunately, however, the sequence of events is clear enough to keep these imprecisions at a reasonably safe distance. And at the very birth of the form we have an opportunity to make useful distinctions, in comparing the contributions of the founding fathers, Strindberg and Chekhov. The flavour of the kind of drama I have in mind has been described by Milkhail Kedrov, where he says of Chekhov's characters that 'their desire for a better life grows stronger as circumstances deteriorate; it becomes finer and concentrated under pressure, the juice of an orange after it has been squeezed'. That's a viable interpretation, but one I'd rather not lean on for my present purpose. It could apply to many masterpieces of the past, including perhaps *King Lear*. Also, Chekhov's characters keep up a good deal of contact with the society around them. But in one case Chekhov does exert pressure on a character in a way that can't be contested, because it is expressed in the choice of location as laid down in the stage directions. The first act of *Uncle Vanya* takes place in a garden, the second in a dining-room, the third in a drawing-room and the fourth in his office, which is also his bedroom. To that extent he is progressively hemmed in.

It is nothing, of course, compared with what had happened to Strindberg's Captain, put in a strait-jacket in full view of the audience. That was in *The Father* (1887), and much could be said of the pressurization in Strindberg. But in terms of this form's later development the key work is *The Dance of Death* (1901), because it spares us from discussing 'impact', 'intensity' and other qualities difficult to present as evidence. The setting and the characters do the job for us. Part One of the play takes place in 'a round fort built of granite'. In the background 'a gateway, closed by swinging double doors' adds to the prison effect. The characters are more cut off from society than Chekhov's, and not only because the protagonist is in the army. They have the long Swedish winter to contend with and the fort is on an island, literally insulated.

The theme is marriage as a love-hate relationship, and it isn't rhetorical if we claim that Strindberg regards marriage as a ghastly solitary confinement 'à deux'. The wife confirms the message given by the setting when she says, 'I have spent a lifetime in this tower, locked up'. The emotional pressure generated is defined by a visitor who says the place is 'so filled with hatred that one can hardly breathe'. As audiences we are being worked on explicitly by insulation and high emotional pressure, not to mention their disturbing connotations – madness, prison. Elements of naturalism, symbolism and expressionism are present, but none of these categories meets the case. The assault on us is a premeditated one, in a new form which needs a new name.

The course of compressionism could be summed up as history falling into line with Strindberg's tortured vision. Not until the diffusion of films and literature about Second World War concentration camps, did the English appreciate his idiom to any extent. The French, having experienced them at first hand, were earlier on the wavelength, starting with *Huis-Clos* in 1944, forty-three years after *The Dance of Death*. What happened in the long interval, apart from two world wars? In this new form of drama, a few dispersed experiments, some of them very significant, until around 1930. Then nothing until Sartre, though plenty was incubating. Both periods have to be examined, however. In 1910 something turns up in a most unlikely quarter, of all people, Galsworthy. *Justice* is a rigidly schematic humanitarian play about a clerk imprisoned for embezzlement. As a protest it succeeded in forcing a reform of the penal code. The bone of contention was solitary confinement, illustrated by a short scene in the third act. The function of the scene is to convey claustrophobia. There is no dialogue, but the stage directions are precise. They require a cell thirteen feet long by seven feet wide by nine feet high and they require the clerk to walk 'like an animal pacing its cage'.

In practice that has to be done by an inset let down from the flies. You get an inner framework within the outer one of a box set, and the effect is like that of Francis Bacon with his inner rectangle. Galsworthy is defining his action in a demonstrable manner for a demonstrable purpose, altering its form. Not that of naturalism, if we are to call the rest of the play naturalistic, not that of expressionism, unless we are to deny that word any precision. No, he is hemming the clerk in, preparatory, as it happens, to having him blow his top. When a theatrical form has become the common property of Galsworthy and Strindberg, it can be regarded as having taken on an independent existence. And that was in 1910. As you'd expect, O'Neill, the acknowledged disciple of Strindberg, was soon aiming for effects of constriction. I must emphasize that stage directions are vital to our documentation. They by-pass the problems of measuring emotional response and they give clues to the dramatist's formal concept, the shape

POPE III
by Francis Bacon, 1951

he was looking for. *The Hairy Ape* (1922) describes the unhinging of Yank, a virtuoso stoker on an ocean liner. The first scene is in the fireman's forecastle, a location about which O'Neill knows all there is to know, but, he demands, 'The treatment of this scene, or of any other scene in the play, should be by no means naturalistic'. About what it ought to be, he is just as explicit: 'The effect sought after is a cramped space in the bowels of a ship, imprisoned by white steel. The lines of bunks, the uprights supporting them, cross each other like the steel framework of a cage.' Two years later *All God's Chillun* develops the process further. The set is made to press in on the Negro student married to a white woman. The first scene of the second act takes place in their New York apartment. For the second scene, and I quote from O'Neill's stage directions, 'The walls of the room appear shrunken in, the ceiling lowered'. For the third, 'The walls of the room appear shrunken still more, the ceiling now seems barely to clear the people's heads'.

So far we have been watching the growth of a new form in terms of major dramatists, conscious of their powers. In 1928, however, the form produced a biological sport, namely *Journey's End* by R. C. Sherriff, devised in the first place for amateur actors at a rowing club. The entire action takes place in a dug-out on the Western Front, enclosed and tense. Sherriff had hit on an objective correlative for the fighting soldier's life in the First World War. Apart from the fitness of the setting, it precipitates neurotic rages in Captain Stanhope, the central character. They are the more effective from being boxed in. Although its revival on television was well received thirty years later by a generation in tune with the idiom, *Journey's End* is an imperfect example of it. The dug-out is as much a refuge as a prison. Dialogue and characterization often reduce the tension generated. All the same, *Journey's End* proves that the idiom can function without the words and people supplied by a major writer, that its particular kind of dramatic life can subsist on a happy choice of situation and visual context, that it is viable at an everyday level of theatrical activity. In an art with one foot on the heights and another in the market place, effectiveness on the lower level is

4

important. For a new form, it is an additional claim to independent existence. And it was at this modest level that compressionism survived during what I have called its incubation period, from around 1930 until 1944. The heroine of a thriller, locked in with a murderer several miles from the village–that was the kind of thing.

More ambitiously, the tower had been bequeathed by the symbolist poets, but as a grey eminence in which the mind expands, not as a prison. Hence the lighthouse, supervised by a disillusioned thinker, in Ardrey's *Thunder Rock*. During the thirties the future of the form we are tracing lay elsewhere, in the grim reality of totalitarian persecution and its literature, that is, in Malraux and Koestler. Before compressionism could be taken seriously, suspense drama and the literature of confinement had to be brought together. That was done by the Nazi occupation of France.

Back in 1935, Malraux's *Le Temps du Mépris* had centred on an intellectual in a Nazi prison. I think a direct line of continuity can be assumed between that novel and the plays of Sartre. The most obvious link is with *Morts sans sépultures* (1946), a study of resistance fighters held in a loft lit by a skylight and waiting to be tortured. For this play to get across, it is unnecessary for the audience to be aware of the author's deeper concerns. It works as Grand Guignol, and was enjoyed as such in translation by audiences at a cinema in Kilburn. The earlier *Huis-Clos* of 1944 is of greater formal interest. Now we are in an existentialist Hell, with only four characters–three prisoners and a gaoler. They are in a Second Empire salon, which has neither windows nor mirror, and they are there for ever. The political activist obsessed by an act of cowardice, has a question to ask: 'Where are the instruments of torture?' These appear soon enough, as his fellow prisoners, a nymphomaniac and a lesbian. They torture one another, simply by being themselves. Here Sartre has removed overt violence from the formula and he has imprisoned his characters not only externally but within their own personalities. And he has added the monotony, the horrible continuity of prison life. The title has been translated into English both as *No*

Exit and *Vicious Circle.* In terms of our definition, by no means loose in this case, insulation is almost complete—the gaoler only answers the bell when he feels like it—and the conflict of attitudes has the focus of ruthless logic.

Since then the form has become a favoured means of expression at various levels of ambitiousness. In 1943, before *Huis-Clos*, the wide, airy focus of the musical *Oklahoma* was narrowed to an inset representing the villain's hut. 'A small window lets in a little light, but not much.' Bresson films a resistance leader in prison; other directors show men trapped in submarines, and so on. Bridget Boland stages the brainwashing of a cardinal. Professor Pevsner draws attention to the sinister recessions devised by Tintoretto. A sense of confinement, no doubt with Kafka's influence active, becomes a cliché. Describing his firemen in *The Hairy Ape*, O'Neill had insisted, 'The ceiling crushes down upon them. They cannot stand upright.' And now Camus's narrator in 1955, compares the human condition to the posture of a medieval prisoner in the 'little-ease', 'not high enough to stand up in nor yet wide enough to lie down in'.

Both Ionesco and Beckett, in *Les Chaises* and *Fin de Partie* (*Endgame*), echo the Strindbergian fortress we met with in *The Dance of Death*. That of *Les Chaises*, also on an island, has circular walls and a monumental double door. Significantly perhaps, the waters below are stagnant. There is no longer any allusion to France or to prison. The doors are stately. Strindbergian rages and the horrors of persecution have gone, and with them the high emotional pressure, the equivalent of a scream. Between the characters there is no conflict worth mentioning. They are basically passive, and appropriately so since the author has described his theme as 'nothingness'. One synonym of 'compress' is 'condense', and these people are as evanescent as exhalations from the waters. Clearly this is an extreme refinement of the form we are discussing. *Endgame*, on the other hand, could be regarded as a mannered version. The windows of the bare, grey interior are so high that they can only be reached by a step-ladder. The posture of the little-ease has been distributed. Clov can't sit and Hamm can't stand. 'Outside,' we are told, 'it's death.' The torture is impersonal, a process of mortality without suspense or screams. Martin Esslin calls this 'a claustrophobic interior', though that is not insisted on in the stage directions or text, except for one thing: Hamm's parents appear, now and then, from ashbins covered with a sheet.

At this extreme you may begin to suspect that compressionism is on its way out. In *The New Tenant* (1956) Ionesco had gone as far as you can in visual enclosure, by ending with his chief character out of sight, 'completely walled in' by furniture, and then by planks let down from the flies. Lastly in Beckett's *Happy Days*, the heroine is imprisoned in a mound of earth up to the waist, Act One–up to the neck, Act Two. All these are mannerisms, gimmicks. Ionesco's encroaching furniture is a comment on materialism, but also pop art, like the congested cabin in *A Night at the Opera*, the crowded room in *The Caucasion Chalk Circle*. All these are comic demonstrations, variety acts with the pressure withdrawn. The urgency of O'Neill, Sartre and Strindberg is miles away. In Beckett it has become conceptual and static, the framework for recitation to a coterie audience. Even in the work of Pinter, one of the best of all practitioners, you see the form breaking up. His two murderers in *The Dumb Waiter* are totally insulated in a dingy bedroom, awaiting orders. Aston and the tramp of *The Caretaker* are psychologically trapped by their personalities and visually by the set, but the third man remains a visitor from outside. The title of *A Night Out* speaks for itself. Somebody calls the hero 'compressed', a play on the word 'depressed' apparently. This was referred to in a notice of the play in *The Times* of 3rd October 1961, which also alludes to 'compressionism' defined as 'the groping of lost souls in a single room'. The only previous use of the term I know of was in a talk on the Third Programme in December of the year 1960.

Mannerisms point to a growing lack of conviction in using the form, while impulses towards epic drama and open staging also work against it. Its immediate future may well be on television. But a hint of its quality can be had from comparing *Huis-Clos* with the film version, opened and loosened by exterior sequences. I have tried to define compressionism rather than evaluate it, though it has already lent itself to original and stimulating work. It has respectable links with the unities of time, place and action, aids to compact construction harped on by Aristotle. It uses the public theatre of its time – that is, the proscenium stage – in such a way as to benefit from architectural limitations. It has been conditioned also by individual genius and the facts of history. I think one may conclude from the evidence that it is a mode of transmission distinct from all others.

The Background

By the time we reach new drama of the nineteen-sixties, the attempt to describe new work in old terminology often becomes too clumsy to be worth the trouble. Aristotle was demonstrably not thinking of plays like *Mother Courage*, *Serjeant Musgrave's Dance*, *Endgame* and *The Brig* when he forged the critical tools which shine bright in the *Poetics* and are still at work today in the popular press, like rusty old spanners which can do little more than gum the works. To use them where they no longer fit either drama theory or practice is academic in a bad sense. It's the negation of reputable scholarship to restrict enquiry to the limitations of the tools available when the tools are obsolete. I take it that the function of criticism is to promote discriminating enjoyment of works of art, including plays. If this is to be done, it's useful to have names for the form a playwright works in, the formal envelope he uses as a means of communication, if you like, the package. But it's useless to go around with a supply of packages never intended to hold the product.

There are, however, two recent packages with labels that stick. In other words they demonstrably describe what playwrights are doing in such matters as narrative, dialogue, subject, conflict and setting. As critical tools they are both abstractions related to artistic facts, and therefore they can serve as a lubricant in discussion rather than promoters of friction. One of them applies to *Mother Courage* and *Serjeant Musgrave's Dance*, the first of the four modern plays I mentioned earlier. It is epic drama, which can be back-dated not only as far as Shakespeare's histories but to medieval mystery cycles. If we think of Brecht as the inventor of it we are mistaken, but he was the first to make us aware of it. The other package is exactly suited to the third and fourth plays listed, *Endgame* and *The Brig*. In the preceding chapter, I pointed out the existence of this dramatic form, demonstrated its characteristics and gave it a name, a label for the package in fact. Since it had not been previously detected and since abstractions ending in 'ism'—realism, naturalism, expressionism—are all prone to misuse through loose definition, I was particularly anxious to justify the new label and to make it stick. So I based my argument mainly on plays, and on the limited amount of those plays which can be judged from the printed text, and within that again, on the evidence of the author's own stage directions. Even dialogue, often the guts of a play, can be debatable evidence because of the way it can be variably coloured in delivery. It is in stage directions that you look for easily demonstrable and irrefutable internal evidence, in the author's own words. There he commits himself to a statement of his intentions. From that rigidly objective foundation I went on to point out relations between the new form and its historical, social and literary context. Now I propose to work in the opposite direction, from life to the theatre. The theatre is a public art which goes limp when it loses contact with everyday life, or with life as reflected in the other arts. A new form that appears in the drama is not in the first place a result of backstage experiment, anxiety or boredom, like the so-called 'theatre of cruelty', but a response to the human predicament. Up to a point, the new form will be historically conditioned.

Anyone in the future who is looking for a concise guide to the flavour of the twentieth century will find it in four brief lines in W. B. Yeats's *Nineteen Hundred and Nineteen*:

> *We are closed in and the key is turned*
> *On our uncertainty; somewhere*
> *A man is killed or a house burned*
> *Yet no clear fact to be discerned.*

This refers to the Irish Civil War, a minor skirmish compared with other wars that have affected everybody, but as Yeats was a great poet the lines are representative. They could be about a dug-out in Flanders, a forward observation post at Stalingrad, a strongpoint in the Congo or a jailhouse in the American South. Their theme is uncertainty, another name for anxiety. The situation is one of confinement and awareness of violence going on outside. The actual location is a ruined tower in Ireland, where Yeats is writing the lines. It symbolizes a retreat for the artist, above and apart from the struggle. Indeed the volume which includes this poem is called *The Tower*, and the tower had become a recurring symbol in literature and life. Not only Yeats but Strindberg and the psychologist Jung lived in homes with towers as a prominent feature. What sets Yeats's lines apart is the feeling that the retreat has become a fortress and an insecure one at that. Part of the uncertainty comes from not being sure how long it will continue to be a refuge rather than a prison. The key is turned all right, but on whose side of the door, inside or out? This makes all the difference, and any doubt we may have is resolved by the fact that Yeats is thinking of an outstandingly terrifying episode in Dante's *Inferno*. It concerns the traitor Ugolino of Pisa, imprisoned with his sons and watching them die one by one. The Belsen touch is that Ugolino's own hunger, not his grief, becomes his ruling sensation. He is bestialized by the experience. It begins with the sound of a turning key:

> *Ed io sentii chiavar l'uscio di sotto*
> *Al' orribile torre*

Meditations in Time of Civil War was written in 1922, a decade before the Nazis came to power. Sometimes the intuition of a great artist like Yeats registers the onset of a vast alteration in human affairs before the event. What he experienced and foreshadowed by way of the poetic imagination was about to be undergone at first hand by the victims of totalitarianism, including intellectuals, that is people with the equipment necessary for analysing and reporting what had happened to them if they survived. For many reasons, too, intellectuals were priority victims of the new barbarism which broke loose in the nineteen-thirties. This barbarism, the rough, slouching beast referred to in another poem, was later to be called 'The New Neanderthal' by Arthur Koestler in *Darkness at Noon*, only he is referring to an embodiment, not to an inspired poetic fiction. By 1940 the fiction has become representative fact and the writer has ceased to be a prophet and become a survivor. But both use related symbols to describe the enemy and neither would regard the horrors of Ugolino's tower as a remote nightmare from the Middle Ages any longer. They have become a commonplace in the concentration camps of Hitler's Germany and Stalin's Russia. Confinement, intuition with Yeats and obsession with Kafka, having first declared itself in the arts, has begun to steal into the human consciousness everywhere, a universal threat. Now, about a quarter of a century after the publication of *Darkness at Noon*, the sense of it is as strong as ever. One of our guides to it is psychology, dealing with the things inside us which go out to meet it and help to close us in. Another guide is the survivor, who reports among other things on external conditions, the means of confinement. What does it feel like to be in prison?

Koestler's hero is Rubashov, a leader of the Bolshevik revolution liquidated in the Stalinist purges. He is fictitious, we're told, but the conditions are real. And from the reactions of Rubashov to these conditions, let us examine just one chain of sensations. At one point, he is lying alone in his cell after a man has been dragged down the corridor outside to execution. When this happens the inmates give the victim support in the only way they can, by drumming on the doors of their cells. Rubashov, 'still had the drumming in his ears, but the silence was now a true silence, empty and relaxed'. Before the execution, 'the silence outside was so thick that he heard it humming in his ears', then 'it was a silence which had swallowed all sound and smothered it, a silence vibrating like a taut drum-string'. Just as the concept of a taut silence followed by a relaxed silence describes his sensations in terms of changes of pressure, without actually using the word, so his awareness of the prison community outside his cell is described later, explicitly in terms of pressure: '. . . the silence became so intense that it seemed to hum and sway. What were the two thousand men doing who were walled in to the cells of this human bee-hive? The silence was inflated by their inaudible breath, their invisible dreams, the stifled gasping of their fears and desires. If history were a matter of calculation, how much did the sum of two thousand nightmares weigh, the pressure of a two-thousandfold helpless craving?'

When Rubashov is given his third interrogation, it is by the method which combines a bright light with deprivation of sleep. We hear of 'the pressure on his eye-sockets brought about by the reflector'. All these passages are describing sensations; the imagery clusters around a dominant feeling. It affects eyes, ears, breathing. The silence varies in density, from empty to thick. It can be relaxed or tense. It can hum, it can go off balance. Just how concentrated the writing is you can tell from the metaphor of the bee-hive, which echoes the idea of humming, and implies something in common between a bee-hive and a prison, both cellular. And there's the relationship between vibration and humming, movement producing sound. Much of the prose in the book is conceptual and rather slack, an exchange of ideas between thinly characterized types who are little more than sign-posts to the route taken by history. So the sensory passages are notable. They seem to reflect intimate, personal experience. When it comes to describing the two thousand walled-in prisoners, Koestler's imagery works two ways to convey a feeling of suffocation. The prisoners 'inflate' that variable silence by their breathing, and the breathing itself is stifled. Nightmares and the working of the lungs are in conflict. To quote Yeats again, this time from as far back as 1919, 'the nightmare rides upon sleep'. But it's interesting to notice that the climax of Koestler's description is a question, like something from an examination paper. We're invited to do a sum about weight and pressure. Even without the final modulation to quantitative imagery, it's obvious that sensations of pressure govern his treatment of this aspect of prison life.

How far is this awareness of atmosphere peculiar to Koestler? His metaphors charge the fact of confinement with an active

oppressiveness, variable and calculable. Our first reaction may
be that we don't need this expert survivor to tell us that any
prisoner must feel closed in. Here we would be mistaken, however, because the account of another equally expert survivor,
Christopher Burney, includes absolutely nothing about the
sensations of confinement as such, nothing claustrophobic.
Clearly the type of person imprisoned counts for a lot. But if any
suspicion remains that Koestler's awareness is exceptional, rather
than typical of our time, it can be put at rest by the testimony of
a third survivor, Eugene Heimler. Describing what it was like in
a ghetto under the Nazis, he writes 'The Yellow Star in 1944 was
intended to degrade us. Personal contacts were severed; it was
now dangerous for a Gentile to walk down the street with a Jew.
Our pride hurt, we could be nothing but proud, sometimes with
reason, and sometimes without. By the end of April I became
aware of an uncanny feeling of being closed in, not by bars or
guards, but by those who lived in that other half of the world. I
felt as if I were in a cage, and night after night I dreamed of
breaking out.' In this case the intuition of Yeats, and the imagination of Koestler, writing from direct experience, has become
premonition. Not long afterwards Heimler was in a concentration
camp, but hallucinations of enclosure had come before the fact.
The process of infiltration into the European consciousness seems
to be as follows. First, a poetic genius arrives at what turns out
to be one of the master symbols of our time, imprisonment and
uncertainty combined. I could have cited Kafka instead of Yeats,
but the links of the process with drama can be shown quite easily
without much probing into the psychology of claustrophobia. So
I will add just one example as a reminder that Yeats isn't alone
among poets in reporting a feeling of enclosure:

> *La prison ouvre sur une prison*
> *Le couloir ouvre un autre couloir . . .*
> *Rien ne débouche nulle part.*

These lines by Michaux are quoted by an expert on Kafka who
says that the images in them at once evoke Kafka's world. Anyway, they clearly express the twentieth-century awareness of

being boxed-in, an awareness which seems to be different from that of other centuries, at least if we are to judge from its manifestations in literature.

Second, in the process of infiltration, come the survivor's reports. The effect of these has been to make exceptional experiences a matter of general knowledge. And this knowledge infects us with anxiety, because recent history has made it only too clear that imprisonment, along with systematically inflicted uncertainty, is no longer as exceptional as it used to be. On the contrary, it is the accepted policy of totalitarian government. Once we know that the articulate survivors are describing the experiences of several million victims, we see their predicament in a new and disturbing light. It could so easily have been our predicament too. And if it could have been in the very recent past, why not in the near future? Why not tonight? Oh yes, we soon begin thinking, it could happen to me.

What you might call the collective imagination is not going to be widely and directly affected by literature on the level of Kafka, or even by survivors with enough imagination to do justice to their theme. Before we can call the new form of anxiety anything as clear cut as 'modern man's prison complex', we need to show that the infiltration does not come to a stop with the intelligentsia but spreads into the everyday interests of people in general. Rather than dig into the mountains of evidence supplied by films and television, I will confine myself to an incident in *Goldfinger*, by the late Ian Fleming. At the end of Part Two, James Bond, the secret agent, has fallen into the hands of the villain: 'I propose to wring the truth out of you,' says Goldfinger, and gives an order to his brutal Korean bodyguard: 'Oddjob. The Pressure Room.' The next chapter, the first in Part Three, is entitled THE PRESSURE ROOM; and we may note in passing that a practised writer is not likely to use the same three words so close together, as a narrative climax, a chapter heading and a bridge between two parts of a three-part novel, unless he is confident that they can carry a high charge of suspense. After an abortive counter-attack, Bond is overpowered. Figuratively speaking 'the whole house fell on him'. He regains consciousness tied to a table with a reflector shining in his eyes. Although the main threat of torture comes from an advancing circular saw, the pressure theme is kept up explicitly, first by the Korean: 'A pressure here, combined with a pressure there, a sudden squeeze, a pause and then a quick, sharp blow.' Eventually Bond remembers something told him by a friend who had survived the Gestapo and he decides that his only hope of withholding information from Goldfinger will be to suffocate himself. His attempt is described in terms of blood-pressure, oxygen, and the resolve to become a vacuum. But 'still the light burned red through his eyelids. Still he could feel the bursting pressure in his temples. Still the slow drum of life beat in his ears'. The links here with the sensory imagery of *Darkness at Noon* are surprisingly close. Compared with Koestler's, the writing is muddled and diffused. Fleming is out to exploit a certain kind of experience for entertainment purposes rather than to master it. Nevertheless, both narratives are founded on an area of fear which has taken on characteristics peculiar to our time. To recognize it in a best-seller novel is to find that it is no longer a minority's concern but everybody's. Two of its running symbols, for some time a cliché, combine in a formula which can be summed up as 'the cage and the scream'. Advance publicity for the film version of *Goldfinger* included a still of Oddjob screaming against a background of iron bars.

Three conclusions emerge from the string of examples I have been discussing. The first is that literary metaphor has repeatedly been organized for describing prison experiences in a manner peculiar to the twentieth century. Second, there is a crystalliza-tion of metaphor around concepts of pressure, expressed in scientific terms, more or less; not surprisingly, in times when science has so often been misused to coerce the individual. Thirdly, the metaphors and the feelings related to them are in general currency. When the means of conveying an experience exist, and the public is attuned to the experience concerned, you have the pre-conditions of drama. Now, what are the drama's means for dealing with boxed-in anxiety, modern man's prison complex? The basic, the simplest–though not by a long way the easiest–is what one actor, on a bare stage under a spotlight, can do to hold the attention of a theatre audience without even speaking. The item in Marcel Marceau's mime repertoire called *La Cage* lasts about ten minutes. Marceau begins by sketching in the walls of his prison. He raises his right hand, palm forwards to indicate immovable resistance, first towards the audience, then towards the prompt corner, then upstage and then to his right, walking several paces each time. After that he walks along an invisible row of iron bars, testing them. Next, he adopts a curious, cramped posture in the centre of the stage and indicates a very small prison within the first. The interesting thing about this contracted prison is that it seems to be in his mind. The other was big enough to walk around in. Anyway, the pool of light contracts too. Presently, he manages to prise two of the bars apart and squeezes through. The pool of light expands. Marceau raises himself up from his hunched position and spreads his arms wide in a memorable gesture of liberation. This turns out to be premature. He finds he is still confined after all. Once again he builds up a prison big enough to walk in, and he ends up as before, closely hemmed in, back in the centre of the stage in a diminishing circle of light. Did he really get through the bars, only to reach an outer wall? Or was he closely trapped all the time? Was the entire partial escape subjective? After only two viewings I don't pretend to know. But study of the lighting plot, without any other evidence, would be enough to convince us that here is drama of a special category.

All this, it should be stressed, has been done without two of the basic elements of the drama: dialogue and scenery. Obviously the prison metaphor can be, and in fact many times has been, reinforced by the spoken word as a means of conveying what happens to the human mind in confinement. Equally obviously the stage itself, at any rate in a proscenium theatre, can be boxed in on three sides, supplied with iron bars, left with no windows at all, or very small ones. In addition, the dynamics of claustrophobia can be enlisted by progressively filling the set with furniture or reducing the size of the set as the action goes forward. The line of development stretches from Ibsen and Strindberg, by way of O'Neill and even *Journey's End*, to Beckett and Pinter.

Proscenium drama is often discussed in terms of an imaginary fourth wall, through which we are supposed to be witnessing what goes on. Surely the process of enclosure must stop there? Not at all. In *The Brig*, by Kenneth H. Brown, the fourth wall itself is explicit and we see the entire action through prison bars. Incidentally, as in Marceau's mime, there is an inner enclosure as well. *The Brig* is a collector's piece to illustrate the dramatic form we are discussing, a beautiful study in the interplay of visual, auditory and psychological pressures, located in an American Marines punishment compound. Hysteria is one of the classic reactions to pressure, and *The Brig* includes a memorable scream.

From all the evidence, of which I have examined only two examples here – *The Cage* and *The Brig* – it is undeniable that the drama has evolved a form, a package, to convey this particular order of experience. It may even be that the drama is better fitted than other arts to convey it intimately and directly. In any case, we expect the arts to keep abreast of human preoccupations, and in return we expect scholars and critics to keep abreast of the arts. They cannot do this without resorting to critical terminology, including abstractions like 'tragedy' and 'comedy', for the sake of convenience and a lucid exchange of ideas. Only this terminology needs to be continuously reviewed and, if necessary, added to. The form evolved to express our prison complex has been in circulation for more than half a century, and it was about time it had a label. We can narrow the gap between criticism and the facts of creative activity if we call this form Compressionism. It concerns itself with compressibility, that is, 'the resistance of materials to stress'.

The Decline

In September 1964, *The Observer* published an article about the British on holiday in Majorca, and in it a foreman at an aircraft factory was reported as follows:

'It stones you. The first two days your British fellow comes out here, it really knocks him for six, he creeps about, you know, don't know what hit him. And then, suddenly, it's like a great weight being lifted off you that's been pushing you down all your days.'

What this man was describing, of course, is a sense of his compressibility. The imagery he uses resembles that of Koestler in *Darkness at Noon*, where the political prisoner Rubashov asks himself how much two thousand nightmares weigh. Both of them are concerned with the resistance of human material to stress, a traditional concern of the arts, but their sensations are typical and appear to be peculiar to the twentieth century, and it's not surprising that the arts have come to develop a new form, compressionism, which cannot only convey the sensation in verbal and visual terms – by showing an hysterical woman trapped in an elevator, for example – but can give the idiom a scientific, or quasi-scientific, sanction.

Unless there is a strong impulse of personal or imaginative experience behind such work, you would expect it sooner or later to slide into a facile and mannered use of the idiom, rather than a powerful use of the form itself, which at its best – in, say, *The Dance of Death* or *Huis-Clos* – can transmit the maximum of con-

THE BRIG
Mermaid Theatre, 1964

flict in a most economical way. Any decline would be aggravated by two factors: the cheap production budget in the theatre of small casts in a single decor, and the hunger of the mass media for drama material. If we consider recent examples of compressionism in television, cinema and the theatre, the form's misuse is evident, but also by implication its original strength.

Its ultimate home, for obvious reasons of intimacy in a small frame, would appear to be television. Quite a good example was *The Devil and John Brown*, based on the fate of a Scottish miner trapped alone by a fall of rock in 1853. Ken Taylor took this theme well beyond the suspense to be had from isolation and the dangers of crushing, by enlisting the victim's puritan conscience to keep up his incredible resistance. When the solitary miner uttered the words 'All of us trapped', he was voicing the familiar compressionist view of the human condition. The familiar devices, and not much else of interest, were illustrated by Rod Stirling's entry for the Italia Prize of 1963, which trapped five ridiculously assorted people in a doorless, windowless, cylindrical prison cell. For this half-hour playlet it could only be said that it was mainstream as to formula and setting, just as encroaching fungus in John Brown's mine echoed the Paris avant-garde. But for rock-bottom use of facile symbolism I could cite another television play where two lovers in adjoining rooms of a mental home clasp hands through the window bars. No doubt any viewer could compile an immense dossier of these disasters. On the whole I prefer the stock, domesticated thriller version of the form, with no play for prison symbolism or cosmic significance, in which an attractive housewife is trapped in her own home by a criminal or a psycho on the run. Will her liberator be the postman, the chatty neighbour or a market research pollster? This type can be called the Who'llstopit, as opposed to the Whodunit, but much of the suspense is drawn from a feeling of enclosure, as in a more sophisticated type centred on persecution by telephone.

Compared with television's output, that of the cinema, to go no further back than *Ivan the Terrible*, *Kanal*, and Olivier's *Hamlet*, was once impressively mainstream, even if we leave explicit treatment of prison subjects out of account. Lately,

5

however, the impulse has given many signs of wearing thin. I can think of equally many reasons for it, among them the trend towards wide-screen, spectacular use of exteriors in colour and towards increasing length. The longer a film runs the harder it is for it to stay in one place without loss of tension. Hence, in 1964, Sidney Lumet's version of *Long Day's Journey into Night* is an evident exception to the rule that the cinema now makes haphazard and capricious use of the idiom of enclosure with little formal coherence. O'Neill, when he chose, was a master of compressionism in direct line from Strindberg, but the extraordinary thing about Lumet's film is that it extracts that form from a play which was not designed in it, except in the sense that O'Neill's tortured family have effectively made their home a prison. Where this film moves more tightly into the form than its original, by the most rigidly concentrated camerawork, most others diffuse and expand. Advance publicity of *The Caretaker*, for example, emphasized the physical confinement, chiefly one room, in which the film was shot, but the result was often exaggeratedly cluttered, with a conscious artistry that distracted one from the fact of confinement. Added to some vaguely desolate exteriors, this, oddly enough, made the tramp and the two brothers appear less boxed-in than they do in the wider spaces of a theatre set.

With Hitchcock's *The Birds*, I think we are down a peg, to a level of brilliantly inventive sensationalism. After long, airy, open passages of drives round the bay, there's a progressive closing in. Tippi Hedren gets attacked in a telephone box, where the birds beat against the glass in their swooping dives and finally break it. The final sequence gathers everybody who matters into one house. They board up the windows as the birds mount their big offensive and at length Tippi Hedren faces a breakthrough alone, upstairs in the attic. I don't think the inventiveness and virtuosity need blind us to the fact that the appeal of all this is novelettishly sadistic in the tradition of romantic agony. Unlike the art of prison survival, it has nothing of consequence to say about the human condition. At the same time, one can admire the deceptively harmless use of a caged bird in the placid, earlier episodes. I suppose it is meant to become the film's controlling image.

In *Goldfinger*, I'm afraid, it's a waste of time to look for anything so consistent. Even by comparison with its original, the film is a riot of loosely contrived imagery. From Ian Fleming's service in wartime intelligence you would expect him to be in touch with the central facts of political imprisonment which led to new work in the arts and a form to convey the experience. And, indeed, in the novel *Goldfinger*, so he is. In the chapter already cited where Bond is tied to a table and evidently on the point of being bisected by an approaching circular saw, an important part of the treatment is a reflector shining in his eyes and a good deal is made of his pulse rate, 'like the huge panting power plant in the other part of the factory'. When he tried to commit suicide by holding his breath, 'the body's instinct to live manned the pumps and got breath back into the body again'. Here Fleming's imagery, where it concerns the light and the stifled respiration, conveys a representative type of resistance to coercion. In the film, on the other hand, the circular saw has become a laser beam, which dominates the episode. Nothing is made of the physiological reactions insisted on in the book.

As if in compensation, however, the cinema clichés of the idiom are distributed jauntily, almost satirically, through the action. At the stud farm, which is Goldfinger's headquarters for planning his raid on Fort Knox, you get instant enclosure by descending walls at the touch of a button. Bond is found in a cell shadowed by vaguely symbolical bars; then he listens to the conspirators from under an iron grille. When we reach the climax at Fort Knox, there's a visual riot of iron bars and their shadows, so lovingly patterned that they almost detract from the action. And finally, Goldfinger's Korean bodyguard is electrocuted, when his metal hat gets lodged between two of them and he reaches for it. It looks almost a parody of that basic formula, the cage and the scream. But two other sequences are the last word in sophistication. One of the conspirators opts out and is offered chauffeur-driven transport to his destination. Against his wishes, it turns out to be a scrap-yard, where the car is pounded to bits by a mechanical crusher and the debris carefully kneaded into a cube small enough to be driven away in a pick-up. Fascinated by the mechanism of the process, one almost forgets that the conspirator was compacted along with the car. As someone remarks, 'he had a pressing engagement'. After this it's rather a comedown to see a man at Fort Knox crushed to death between iron railings and a door of one of the vaults, but Goldfinger's own fate in a pressurized aircraft cabin reaches top form again. He is sucked out of it through a hole in the fuselage, a case of compression in reverse.

Apart from the ingenious amusement to be had from *Goldfinger*, the film illustrates a lavish breaking up and dehumanization of one of the dominant artistic forms of our time. 'I dislike being cooped up like this', says one of the conspirators, rather casually, when the push-button walls descend. The interest is less in enclosure than the way it is done. Compressionism has become science fiction. To put it in scientific terms, the result of pressure is deformation of material, and the present tendency in the arts, though not as it happens in *Goldfinger*, is to linger over the deformation of human material and take the pressure for granted. I find this morbid and lacking in intensity. For example, the bath-house in the *Marat/Sade* is a showplace, at any rate in Peter Brook's production, for a display of dehumanized, morbid symptoms. Its walls are not in the least oppressive. And similarly, in the later paintings of Francis Bacon the inner framework which used to contain the figures has gone. There are still no doors or windows, but nobody screams any more. Even that reaction would be too positive. Any resistance there may have been is over, and it seems to me that these paintings now describe the results of an experience, where the earlier ones communicated the experience itself.

Perhaps the chief justification for tracing the decadence of an art form is the light thrown backwards on the form in full vigour, before it fell into casual use and weakened from overwork. We can appreciate Strindberg, O'Neill, Eisenstein, and the Bacon of the cardinals, better after noting the effects of their method when it has been split up and indulged in without conviction. But if anyone still doubts that compressionism exists or is uncertain about what can be done with it, a vigorous latecomer, *The Brig*, is a clinching example. The first thing to notice about Kenneth H. Brown's dramatization of imprisonment in the American Marine Corps is a statement made by the author. 'Most theatres', he said, 'go about designing a set to facilitate the actor's job. I force the actor within the limitation which I construct before writing the play.' This is the method of compressionist masters like O'Neill and Strindberg, explicit in their stage directions. There are two ways of reminding oneself how thoroughly Brown pursues it in *The Brig*. One is to glance at the ground-plan in the printed version. A better, perhaps, is to visualize the Mermaid production.

The stage at the Mermaid is a platform, meeting the front row of the stalls and open at the sides, so as to leave two empty areas between the flanks of the platform and the theatre's walls. For *The Brig*, these open sides are enclosed by a false proscenium. Across it stretches a continuous run of widely meshed wire, through which the audience witnesses the play. Between this outer compound and the inner one, in the actual prison, was a concrete wall, which of course has to go. Instead we look through the first run of wire across an open corridor directly into the inner compound, containing twelve prisoners' bunks, wired with narrower mesh. Any last vestiges of open platform the Mermaid ever had are disguised by the side and back walls of the stage areas outside the inner compound. They represent offices for the guards.

With this formal mechanism at his command, Brown doesn't need to insist on the fact of enclosure; it's obvious. But he has a theme which lends itself to elegant compressionist variations. For instance, there's a large rubbish bin, in which one prisoner is ordered to squat, with the lid down, as another hammers the top of it while intoning passages from the training manual. One night a woman walked out at this point, forgetting her mink stole. Less overtly distressing, but more subtly claustrophobic, are the white lines here and there, because the prisoners are conditioned to cross them with ritual formality. A tense climax arrives when the time comes to wash one of these lines. That involves touching it, infringing a taboo. No doubt about the nature of the stresses here, but where's the resistance? Well, quite simply in the youth and toughness of the prisoners under pressure. To that extent it really wasn't so far off the mark when service men in America read the play as a tribute to the resilience of the Marines.

And in fact there is an episode of individual resistance in the best tradition of the cage and the scream. Prisoner No. 26 unexpectedly asserts his identity and objects to being treated like a child. Then he emits a 'terrifying scream'. This is no actor's improvisation or doubtful memory from the audience. I quote from the printed stage directions. At one performance the scream was omitted, with a notable shift in balance and tension. Either way, No. 26 is then beaten up and progressively enclosed still further, first in a barred solitary confinement cell, then in a strait-jacket. So we are back to Strindberg and *The Father* of 1887, where the victim was put in a strait-jacket by his old nurse, who talked to him as if he were a child. At important moments in *The Brig*, the guards also address their prisoners in this way.

I don't think this parallel with Strindberg devalues *The Brig*. On the contrary, Brown's play is a happy marriage of the prison experience with the form best suited to convey it. The treatment is rigidly detached and economical, classically so. To fault it on the grounds that the dialogue is undistinguished is to miss the point, and incidentally, to misconceive the nature of dramatic action. To find it boring, as some critics did, may be only to reveal that one has led a very sheltered life. The fact remains that it did not draw the public, not even the sizeable minority public that goes to the theatre for kicks. Why? Partly because *The Brig* is not sensational in the bad sense. An aspect of the classical element is that it does not present any details of physical malformation. But I suspect that, having arrived so late, *The Brig* suffers undeservedly from the debasement of compressionist idiom which I have already described. Perhaps it couldn't be expected to draw a public sated, in several media, with the imagery of confinement.

Meanwhile awareness of the experience, what it feels like to be boxed-in, weighed-down and so on, if anything seems to have spread. What used to be the preserve of a few articulate victims, spokesman for millions of others, is now common knowledge. From popular compressionism the luckier millions have learnt what happens to isolated man's pulse rate and breathing when the bright reflector is on, what fantasies crowd in on him, alone or in company, in prison. Nobody could call it a comfortable kind of knowledge, but given the history of our times, perhaps the possession of it is now a necessary part of being human. Even in a society free from political persecution it has its uses, not least in a society like ours in which cars and hotel rooms grow smaller, stress is a medical cliché and a foreman on holiday can think of the assembly line as a weight on his chest.

Closed Valley

I have already cited the Beckett of *Endgame* and *Happy Days* as a dealer in mannered compressionism, his characters more and more passive. In *Play*, at the National Theatre, he takes the process of enclosing them another stage further. He has refined the form in one direction as far as it can go, petrified it almost. Samuel Beckett is the most learned of living dramatists. In his case the straight theatre reporting that usually passes for criticism just won't do. We have to dredge up the most remote or the most commonplace memories of things we happen to have read. For example:

> *Can storied urn or animated bust*
> *Back to its mansion call the fleeting breath?*
> *Can Honour's voice provoke the silent dust,*
> *Or Flattery soothe the dull, cold ear of Death?*

The first two lines of Gray's stanza give a fair idea of Beckett's visual method in *Play*. Three urns are side by side on the stage, each with a protruding head. A light picks them out in turn and when it does they speak, fleetingly animated. The answer to the first question, can a memorial urn come to life, is 'Yes' here in the theatre. Provoke is an exact word for the effect the light has on the statuary. It brings them to a fitful, gabbling life, on and off. And the notion of flattery, or anything else, being able to mollify death is foreign to everything we know about Beckett. So the answer to the third question is very definitely 'No'. In many ways he's a very nineteen-twenties writer, never very far away from the symbolist allusiveness of Joyce and Eliot, and this is my excuse for what otherwise could seem a very remote quotation indeed. As follows:

> A: Cicero says that three things distract the mind from love: satiety, shame and reflection. As for shame–tell me, and excuse me, have you looked in your mirror lately? Haven't you noticed that your face is changing, day by day?
>
> B: Now that you mention it, yes. Men seem to get old faster now than they used to.
>
> A: Renounce the follies of youth; extinguish the ardors of adolescence. Don't be forever thinking of what you have been; look around you to realise what you are now.

That dialogue is from Petrarch's *Secretum* (in Morris Bishop's translation). It would surprise me very much to learn that Mr Beckett hadn't read it. The *Secretum* is in Latin, but Italian was one of his BA degree subjects in the twenties. That would bring him close to Petrarch, and during the war Beckett was living for a time in, of all places, the Vaucluse, where Petrarch had his celebrated country retreat. Anyway, the attitude and preoccupations of the *Secretum* are relevant enough to *Play*. Old sexual wounds are throbbing steadily in both.

Of course, there is one way in which Beckett is not at all a nineteen-twenties writer, but a man of the nineteen-forties, indelibly marked by the dangers of the Resistance movement in occupied France, a man obsessed by the idea of confinement. The formal means of expressing this in art is compressionism, hysteria in a closed space. You had it in *Happy Days* with a woman progressively buried up to her neck, and you have it in *Play*, with its volleys of hysterical laughter and trunkless heads. The stage directions insist that the actors inside the urns cannot sit down. They must either kneel or stand. Almost, you might think, the dramatist in the role of an SS man.

But how can a mind like this, experience like this, a temperament so complex and private, be brought to bear in public? On the night I was there the National Theatre audience was completely gripped, though it's all over in around twenty minutes. Well, first, there's the external point of contact, a routine adultery situation between wife, husband and mistress, a shoddy cliché of drama in any medium. Each gabbles out his reaction in turn at incredible speed. For example, I'm indebted to Martin Esslin for the information that they committed suicide. Need the tempo really be so fast? Apparently, yes, because the author was at rehearsals; and if an audience can be held at such a tempo it means that the second point of contact, the essential communication, is subliminal, below the level of consciousness. It works like tightly compressed chamber music that can bear repeated hearings. The acting of Rosemary Harris, Billie Whitelaw and Robert Stephens, under the direction of George Devine, is perfect within the limits prescribed. As you would expect, the strong Royal Court element in the National Theatre knows how to deal with Beckett. But everything contributes to a devaluation of sex, an attitude recurrent in Beckett's work and, in my view, its chief if not crippling, limitation.

3. EPIC

Epic as Drama

When the Wakefield cycle of mystery plays was put on at the Mermaid in 1961, Martial Rose the adapter was asked if he connected medieval drama in a northern dialect with our new vernacular playwrights. His answer was, 'No. I don't see Delaney in it. I see Brecht. It's epic drama. It sweeps in location and in time and cuts across all the classical rules.' So, one might add, do Shakespeare's histories, so do Westerns on the screen and so did three of the most interesting productions of the past few years: the Royal Shakespeare's *Troilus and Cressida*, the Old Vic's *Peer Gynt* and Bristol's *War and Peace*. If we try to assess what is actually happening in contemporary drama and stop trying to pour it into moulds like comedy and tragedy, no longer applicable, then we at once recognize two formal categories poles apart. One is compressionism, an intensification of Aristotelian high pressure, which we have already discussed. The other is epic. Of these two dominant forms, I think epic has more to offer live theatre in the immediate future. Quite apart from its present linking with the name of Brecht, it has a history along the grooves of both high culture and pop. For maturing dramatists today it has three obvious attractions. It can draw on a reservoir of historical material, it's not parochial or domestic, and – a prosaic but important recommendation – epic fits the use which modern directors like to make of their actors, equipment and stages.

Why has this form had so little critical attention on its way to first place in today's theatre? Partly, I'm certain, because of the hundred-year swing of literary taste away from epic. It would need a book to explain that process. There's the peculiar case of Ariosto, for example. In the eighteenth century he is still required reading. Early in the nineteenth Byron and Shelley exult over him and Scott is known as the Ariosto of the North. By the middle of this century the intelligentsia has almost forgotten who Ariosto is, because his business, like Byron's, is to send up the epic, and few people any longer care what the epic is. Well, here is C. M. Bowra's definition of 1945: 'an epic poem is by common consent a narrative of some length and deals with events which have a certain grandeur and importance and come from a life of action, especially of violent action such as war'. Epic drama is the same thing in theatrical terms, but we can't bring it into focus without going back a little to consider that hundred-year eclipse of the form. One thing the epic has never been is chairborne, domestic. But those hundred years were overwhelmingly the years of the middle-class domestic stronghold even in James, even in Proust. They were the years of the novel, of strenuous private reading in the long winter evenings of middle-class leisure, before the invention of radio and later of television broke that pattern up. Whereas the epic presupposes an audience, and its formal divisions chime with what can be read out at a single session, perhaps to a court. In that sense the epic is already on the way towards drama.

Superseded by the novel in literature, the epic ran counter to what was going on in the theatre. There, from the time of Tom Robertson's sets with 'practicable' doors, the tide was running strongly towards a cult of family crises. Morality ruled out the bedroom for serious purposes, leaving the study and the drawing-room. And these are in fact the apt locations for crises of bourgeois life. Here is the flashpoint of conflict, here dirty linen is washed in private. Also it's the citadel of the middle class, the hunter's billet, status symbol and ultimate shelter. We are inclined to forget how bold it was of Chekhov in *The Cherry Orchard* to show a middle-class home being sold up and then dismantled in full view of an audience. But these locations were not only the logical choice for domestic drama. Stage conditions, that is the box set on a proscenium stage, were made to fit them like a glove. For the first time, drama grew to be thought of as something happening indoors, in a living-room. (It went as far as regarding the actor's point of contact with the public as a fourth wall, an extraordinary notion which needs more examination than it has ever had.) At all events, the idea of drama as something happening in a room was deeply rooted for several generations, so deeply that opponents of the new English drama of 1956 discussed it in terms of its location, supposedly just another room, the kitchen. They began to get really worried when compressionist writers – Sartre, Beckett and Pinter – were seen to regard rooms no longer as homes at all, but as torture-chambers and prisons.

Domestic drama – and even *The Three Sisters* and *The Master Builder* are domestic dramas – needs activating if we are not to weary of the accurately observed behaviour induced by the set. Family crises tend to exclude physical action and the primitive joys of story-telling. But they remain crises, and lend themselves to the Aristotelian concept of drama as a tightly coiled spring. Like *Oedipus Rex*, domestic drama depends very much on the disruptive effects of an appalling secret, as Ibsen demonstrated. And to reinforce them came the influence of Freud, whose special field was the appalling secret within a family. From *Hedda Gabler* to *The Connection* domestic drama has relied on depth psychology for the kicks. In the theatre there isn't an enormous difference between a Norwegian scholar's drawing-room and a junky's pad. Neither can offer what we are so fond of calling 'epic sweep'. Neither can accommodate much physical action. Grandeur, if any, is strictly private, as Granville-Barker discovered in the last act of *Waste*, in which the ruin of a politician can leave us with nothing more urgent than an unhappy gentleman in his Queen Anne Street study. This is as far as you can get from epic, although the ruin of a politician is epic material, potentially. As it happens, Granville-Barker's hero is ruined by a more or less appalling secret, and even the outward structure of this kind of play has an inward tendency. Rather than on narrative it relies on plot, which can mean a secret design.

Something in human nature rebels against the rigours of

Aristotelian drama and wants to stretch. Directors like Poel, and Granville-Barker himself, climbed out of the drawing-room on Shakespeare's back. Moreover, the Victorian eclipse of epic drama was never total, because literary epic survives in folk art, in debased versions of tremendous vitality. One example is the Sicilian puppets, still holding audiences today with the exploits of Ariosto's paladins. Another is the very successful film, *El Cid*. My contention is that the popular hunger for myth is of vital importance to drama if it can continue to flourish in areas as remote from one another as Sicilian folk art and wide-screen colour films. But you cannot satisfy the hunger for myth in a boxed-in, everyday domestic setting. During the high-culture eclipse of epic, then, its mobility and expansiveness flowed into melodramas and spectaculars: James O'Neill in *The Count of Monte Cristo*, Matheson Lang in *The Wandering Jew*. I think it was tolerated in Shakespeare but not well understood. If it had been understood, why all that criticism of *Julius Caesar*, an obvious epic, in terms of tragedy? Why all that slowing down of the narrative by overloaded, antiquarian sets?

After the eclipse of epic, its reinstatement. According to Bowra, it is expected to flourish 'at the end of a great historical process'. Although 1914 is generally thought of as such a finish, the progress of epic drama between the wars can only be followed if we continue to keep an eye on both high culture and pop. Domestic plays continued to feed on depth psychology, on character and personal tensions. Literary taste favoured symbolism and the short, complex poem, with close analysis as the feed-back. Expressionism, though it opened up the stage, also leant heavily on depth psychology, which is alien to epic, and its didacticism was more in the foreground than epic homilies ought to be. The first of these expressionist tendencies, the Freudian one, was a handicap to Auden and Isherwood's *The Ascent of F6*. I well remember my disappointment at the Little Theatre in 1936, when the veiled figure on top of the mountain in the last act turned out to be the hero's mother. For an example of irksome didacticism, one need look no further than the songs in Brecht's *The Exception and the Rule*. Here, in expressionism,

Esslin demonstrates in *Brecht: A Choice of Evils*, he was a genius not to be understood from his own statements of policy, and he ended by disowning the label of epic drama. His was a very different temperament from Tasso's but equally tortured, and much of his power comes from the contest with epic discipline. All the fuss about alienation, not Brecht's invention and not capable of being sustained for long in any public assembly, all that search for an impossibly judicial audience, may be read as a bid for objectivity. Marxism, too, can be seen as a frame of reference outside the writer's personality, like Christianity in Tasso or Milton, and the *pax romana* in Virgil. Being more concerned with Marxism than with depth psychology Brecht was inevitably tilted away from the wound-up tens.. of domestic drama towards epic. He was a magnificent story-te.. as good as any the drama has known. *The Caucasian Chalk Cir.. .llows* two long narrative loops, apparently disconnected, but jo.. t the finish. His didacticism is the main blemish: it acts as a bra.. mobility. The same could also be said of his convoluted irony, though that might equally well rank as an enrichment of epic drama. John Arden has taken it over in the last act of *Serjeant Musgrave's Dance* without loss of impetus, whereas in *Luther* and *Chips with Everything* the narrative line bogs down in unresolved problems of individual psychology.

Epic drama is epic put across to a theatre audience. How it is done matters less than an appreciation of the form, but that in turn depends on getting epic off the shelf. The means of production are ready. They include designers thinking in terms of evocative emblems and backgrounds projected swiftly, directors punctuating narrative by changes of light and stressing the narrative contours by concerted action; and actors, hot from location work on *Lord Jim* or *Lawrence of Arabia*, not to be fenced in. The audience is ready, conditioned by the cinema's answer to domestic drama on television, by colour films on a wide screen. So far all this theatrical energy has tended to flow one or other of two ways, towards Artaud's 'theatre of cruelty'—an emotional substitute for structure—or towards epic.

The revival of epic drama could have been traced by arriving

at a synthesis of recent productions. Mostly it has been a conspiracy of interpreters and audiences, by-passing the playwright.
What has epic drama to offer the writer now? Apart, of course,
from directors and actors only too willing to manage without him.
Well, first the structural problems, which I have summed up as
an escape route from obsessions. Secondly, a reservoir of historical subjects, not omitting the English Civil War. Thirdly, its
own built-in antidote: the satirical Ariosto, Berni, Cervantes and
Fielding. And fourthly, there is the vernacular element, folk-lore
or pop. E. K. Chambers identifies characters called Big Head and
Slasher in the mummers' plays. On another level, I suppose one
might add the epic as a means of orientation. It has been one of
man's most useful instruments for locating himself. Of this order
is an inter-war masterpiece I have held in reserve, as a final
reminder of epic drama's existence apart from Brecht. It is *In
Parenthesis* by David Jones, a classic in print and on sound radio,
but not staged yet, though I have no doubt it will find a place in
the repertory of the National Theatre. The central character is
a private soldier of the First World War, one of the long line of
epic anti-heroes.

Arden

As a comment on political strategy *Armstrong's Last Goodnight*, by John Arden, is about a sophisticated courtier who thinks he can manipulate primitive Border chieftains by following the more advanced ideas of European statecraft. His failure is summed up in one line: 'Rationality and practicality has broke itself to pieces'. The Border clans, and notably Johnny Armstrong their archetype, don't react according to the rules. One day a chieftain will be talking of the King of Scotland as if he were a minor competitor, the next he'll be lost in delusions of grandeur at the notion of being called the King's brother. In matters of religion the clansmen are equally inconsistent. If a chieftain can try to cover a recent murder by telling the court that he and his rival are at peace, surely the same man can be relied on to resist an evangelical preacher? Not at all. When a preacher turns up, Armstrong's household change over from tribal ballads to Lutheran chants at the drop of a hat.

In his turn the preacher is infected by the violence of his new protectors, for as soon as his motives are questioned he sinks a knife through the peritoneum of the offender, who happens to be the envoy's loyal friend and secretary. The slow death involved is a good example of the legitimate use of violence on stage. It gives Lindsay a lesson about the forces he has so condescendingly manipulated and it removes the glamour which he has seen in them as a poet. 'You can never accept the gravity of another man's violence,' Lindsay has been told. Having seen his friend die, he finally does accept it, removes the last vestiges of romanticism and humanism from his diplomacy, advocates the imprisonment of the chieftains and has Armstrong hanged, after enticing him to a meeting with the King. Lindsay has learnt that the reality underlying tribal romanticism is a knife in the guts.

The action of the play is framed by the diplomat Lindsay who introduces it and signs it off. He and Armstrong are the main structural pillars, and my main criticism of the National Theatre Company's production is that both of them are weakened. In the case of Lindsay it is a matter of casting. Robert Stephens excels himself. He's unfailingly intelligent and in this part unexpectedly courtly, best of all when composing himself for an audience with the King. To say that Mr Stephens is a natural comedian does not belittle the curious dignity he arrived at in *The Royal Hunt of the Sun* and, briefly, in *Much Ado*. But it's brittle, finely drawn dignity, like that of a greyhound. It might pass for the poet in Lindsay, though not as a physical equivalent of the latter's tone in his verse as we know it. For the calculating seriousness of Lindsay the politician an actor of less agility, less mercurial temperament is needed, the more so because Armstrong is played by Albert Finney with a hypnotic presence which rivets the attention at Chichester while he's seated with his back to most of the audience, and once merely by raising his hand to grip a woman's face. I have not seen this gesture improved on since Massine's hand froze a hot whirl of action by one short movement in his Viennese ballet. Weightier opposition for Armstrong would increase the play's impact.

If one pillar of the action is frailer than seems to be necessary, the other is deliberately toppled over just before the finish by a misapplication of alienation technique. Just as *Sergeant Musgrave's Dance* refers implicitly to Cyprus, so *Armstrong* has parallels with events in the Congo and the moment chosen to hint at them is one that could equally well have been used to give us a final, barbaric taste of Armstrong's glamour. To meet the king he arrives adorned with a selection of his fabulous loot, including— and I quote from the stage directions—'a wide-brimmed hat, turned up over the forehead', on which are pinned a number of jewelled badges after the fashion of Field-Marshal Montgomery's beret. I can't find anything in the stage directions or the surrounding dialogue to indicate that Armstrong is meant to look ridiculous in this get-up. On the contrary it makes nonsense of the primitive grandeur already claimed for him if he does. Yet the effect made by Finney, with the connivance of his directors, is of a farcical savage tricked out in European loot. This may be helpful as a comment on African politics but not as a prelude to the hanging, where Armstrong heroically improvises a Border ballad before they top him.

For a means of comparison some will be indebted to the Glasgow Citizens' Theatre's original production of the play, and myself to Bennett Maxwell's adaptation for the Third Programme. The impediment required for Armstrong's diction is a fatal handicap on sound, where nothing visual can mark him out as a leader; and murder, of course, is reduced to some grunts and a rattle of weapons. But Leonard Maguire's Lindsay comes over with a very satisfactory detachment, merely by giving him an English accent. Arden's lines have everything to gain from native Scottish actors in the other parts, and the radio production is better cast anyway than the Chichester one at three vital points: the King, the evangelist and the tragic female victim. Being shorter, it also concentrates the political thinking.

Comparison of the two productions are in the play's favour entirely. It registers equally as action drama with the basic appeal of a Western movie, or—given a nodding acquaintance with Middle English and the Border ballads—as recited epic. Beyond that it has the coherent political structure which I've already separated out. Lindsay's position in Armstrong's domain is like that of Machiavelli on his mission to Cesare Borgia and Armstrong meets the same fate as the rivals enticed by Borgia to a peace conference. In spite of Geraldine McEwan's quite brilliant performance, I'm not sure what's gained except entertainment by having Lindsay and Armstrong share the same mistress. But the infusion of evangelical religion, as in *Musgrave*, has Arden's signature on it. Perhaps the lack of it pulls down the temperature of his Magna Carta play a little; though not as much as King

John's late and disastrous address to the audience, which takes one back to the early pseudo-Brechtian days of the Royal Court on a Sunday night. Incidentally, Robert Eddison's and Patrick Wymark's acting in *Left-Handed Liberty* ought not to prevent one from admiring the direction at the Mermaid as well. It's by David William, very well grouped and clear in its narrative line. I mention this because Arden has suffered from frivolous and self-conscious directors in his time. Now he's an assured and original epic dramatist, good enough to extend the best actors we can find.

Some of the criticism which *Armstrong* has met with seems to come from inadequate sympathy with epic drama, and indeed from uncertainty as to what epic does. What epic can't do is to accommodate private, esoteric states of feeling or complex analysis of character. From Virgil to screen Westerns, the characters act out the *type* of a Roman, a barbarian, an outlaw or whatever. The generic terms gun-man or law-man are of crucial importance. In this play, we ought to be thinking of political man, clansman, and man of God; and therefore I don't agree with those who think that Finney overdoes the savagery, though I would like to see the King played more like a type and less like a seedy conspirator. The language barrier is another matter; it depends on how far an audience should be made to work. If instant comprehension is the aim, then Arden is taking a risk, but no greater than the one taken by Sir Tyrone Guthrie when he put on Lindsay's *The Thrie Estatis* at Edinburgh, where it was revived year after year. It just happens that the dialogue of *Armstrong* is no barrier to me because my father came from the Border and the ballads were normal reading for me at an early age. Leaving the widely known Burns and Chaucer out of account, there must be a fair number of people who heard the late James McKechnie's unforgettable reading of Dunbar's verse on radio. Rather than question Arden's wisdom in choosing this idiom, we ought to thank him for reminding us of its directness and power. Anyway, it's the kind of undertaking which a National Theatre exists to promote.

In comparison with Arden, Osborne and Pinter remain essentially private, emotional and even domestic writers. Sometimes their later work seems to rise from problems caused by their own success. You remember they were once actors, who now have to examine their creative values in close contact with show-business. After the initial impact of the fifties, the first interesting protest or the first release of powerful obsessions, the writer's alternative to repeat performances is a flirtation with pop or else a more mature understanding of the bigger world outside. Arden has yet to be popular, and one reason why he can handle epic themes may be that he's the only leading dramatist of the fifties who had a university education.

Open Stage

The stage at Chichester is a wedge thrust out among the audience, a number of whom look at the show from a lateral angle across its long sides. Three sides of the platform are open and the fourth is a built-up architectural feature with three main levels. We are not dealing with an arena stage, then, not with the circus or theatre-in-the-round, but with something more like the Greek and Elizabethan theatres, a stage with three sides and a back. For a modern audience the architectural feature at the back is a source of confusion, because it encourages the visual habits we bring to the normal proscenium theatre. In *The Chances* it is left absolutely bare, stripped for action in a picaresque romp. Only, the romp is supposed to happen in Naples and the structure obstinately refuses to take part. It casts a cold, functional eye on all the goings on. It is there when we come in, there in the interval and there when we leave, ostentatiously neutral, like Nelson's column.

For *The Broken Heart* it wears Pompeian fancy dress and for *Uncle Vanya* one wall, with door and windows, of a Russian house. But in all three plays it tends to brood over the platform the way a ship's bridge dominates the quarter deck. It may be no more than the walled-up ghost of the proscenium stage, but it's a nuisance. It swallows up a gay scene in *The Chances*, played on its balcony, and a tragic one in *The Broken Heart*, played underneath. And it reduces the storm in *Uncle Vanya* to a remote grumble and flicker behind a partition. So we are deprived of the anchorage in space we are used to, while the stairs, balcony and catwalk replacing it don't properly register yet. But most of the work is being done on deck, on that rather forbidding-looking platform, the open stage. What's going on there? Perpetual motion, for one thing, some of it ingenious, but a lot of it defiant. *The Chances*, in particular, comes over like a dummy run to make the actors feel at home. Up they come from the foyer, down the stairs from the balcony. The localization so wickedly foisted on us by proscenium stages has gone, and with it some of the reality of the characters. To take examples, the debonair comedy in *The Chances* depends on the two young Spaniards being visitors to Naples, intruders. On the bare stage at Chichester there's no environment for them to intrude on, no residents and no visitors, just actors making appearances on balconies, steps and the platform. Or that's how it seems. And in Ford's tragedy, full of pig-headed existentialists battering out for themselves an identity, there we miss the background of a kingdom which survives them. A few solid, costly-looking objects, an inhabited set, would help. The characters need a springboard for their leaps into self-realization. I'd settle for roughly the same cast in the cool, columnar set used by André Barsacq for Racine's *Bérénice*.

These are strategic considerations, of how far open staging draws the teeth of a picaresque comedy and a baroque tragedy by leaving the action too much adrift. Another strategic consideration is the choice of director. Olivier is not yet a virtuoso director of classical drama like Guthrie or Brook. Either of them would have made something entirely different of both plays in the same theatre. But they would have been up against the same tactical problems, inherent in the open stage itself. First, we are always being told that it is intimate, and on this evidence it's anything but. The nearer you are to the actors, the more obvious it is that they are working very hard to project. From a side view, you might as well be seated in the wings of a proscenium stage. The scale of the acting looks just about the same. In fact, I'm inclined to think that the auditorium at Chichester, with its capacity of one thousand three hundred and sixty, may be around five hundred seats too big for the kind of interaction claimed by open-stage theory.

Apart from that, however, there's another tactical problem, arising from the fact that actors on the platform are continually turning their backs on one segment of the audience in order to address themselves to another. Sir Tyrone Guthrie claims that this need not matter, because the moves can be so arranged that you always have either the speaker or his interlocutor in sight. I think it does and always will matter, and for three reasons. First of all, when an actor has his back to you, you are deprived of his chief means of communication: the look in his eyes. Second, you never know when this turning away is going to happen. It breeds a sense of frustration and insecurity in the audience. And third, revolving actors are bound to produce annoying changes of vocal tone and volume which have no artistic function.

I have avoided entering into one of those foggy discussions about theatrical illusion, because once anybody pretends to be somebody else in public, the illusion is there, whatever the shape of the stage. Nothing in a picture frame is more artificial than two people on opposite sides of an open stage sharing out a conversation scrupulously. (It reminds one of the two tourists separating at the entrance to the Tate Gallery: 'You do the right side, and I'll do the left'.) It seems to me that the theorists have been wrong on at least four counts. They have propagated the fallacy that proscenium stages are more illusionist than others. They have underrated the value of localized action; not many playwrights have Shakespeare's gift of painting a scene in words, and anyway the cinema and television have made us more conscious of environment, not less. The theorists have also confused intimacy with rhetoric. When a less than great actor gets through to us on the open stage – Tom Fleming, for example, in *The Thrie Estatis* – it's as an orator on a platform. What's intimate about that? Above all, a lot has been written on the subject from an antiquarian standpoint, with little or no attention to the needs of a living audience.

At Chichester one of the finest companies ever assembled in this country is testing an egghead theory under laboratory conditions, at great expense. On those grounds alone there ought to be full houses. But what is the outlook for open staging? In spite of its limitations, it offers an outlet for some of the most powerful impulses in present-day drama. Whether these impulses are rational or not is a secondary matter. The impulse of actors and directors is to get physically as near as possible to the public. This is probably an anxiety reaction to the fear of losing audiences, literally, as many companies have lost them, to counter attractions. The impulse of audiences is to have acting magnified in the way they are accustomed to on the screen. Neither of these impulses is any longer met by proscenium theatres, and if I had a financial interest in a proscenium theatre I would view the cult of open staging with great anxiety.

4. REALISM

Aspiration and Dusty Fact

Realism is not a form of dramatic act, but a tendency. It is the name given by dramatists, actors and directors to the gestures they make towards everyday life, and these gestures are important because the theatre is always in danger of being strangled by its own conventions. At the same time, realism is a corrective to fantasy, for fantasy is on the whole personal and private, whereas the theatre is public. But it is one thing to claim that you are practising realism and another to achieve it. Tom Robertson, for example, is often cited as a pioneer realist in England, because he was the first to introduce 'practicable doors' to our stage and because his dialogue was less artificial than that of other mid-Victorian dramatists. This does not prevent his *Caste* (1867) from seeming a charming museum piece now. Although that is an extreme case of its misuse, it may remind us that the word 'realism' often serves as a substitute for thought.

All the same, there are two classic occasions which reveal the tendency, the resolve to close the gap between theatre and life. The first was the *Daily Telegraph*'s hysterical attack on *Ghosts* (1891) and the second was the riot at the première of *The Playboy of the Western World* (1907). Both these plays had smashed the conventions, not structural conventions (we lack the sense of logic which can be enraged by a run-on alexandrine), but agreed rules about what can be tolerated publicly in words and action. Ibsen had based a play on hereditary syphilis and Synge's heroine had shown contempt for a priest. In both cases, the fury of public reaction registered the degree of realism, or at least the former distance between life and drama in London and Dublin. Nineteen years later another riot occurred at the Abbey Theatre, this time as a result of O'Casey's *The Plough and the Stars* (1926). Between Synge and O'Casey came the Irish civil wars. The two riots frame a period. Its influence on realism in the English theatre today is precise and decisive, leading directly to Wesker and Littlewood.

The link was a woman, Miss A. E. F. Horniman (1860–1937), creator of the Abbey Theatre and formerly secretary to W. B. Yeats, a great poet noted for the realistic tendencies of his later work. After leaving the Abbey in 1910, Miss Horniman continued to control the Gaiety Theatre, Manchester, until 1921. Round her there crystallized the Manchester School, described in *The Oxford Companion to the Theatre* as 'realistic plays of provincial life'. One of them, *Hindle Wakes* by Stanley Houghton, is remarkably bold for its time. At the climax a working-class girl, seduced by a mill-owner's son and grudgingly offered marriage, refuses him, in flat contradiction to current social and theatrical convention. Another of the plays, *Hobson's Choice* by Harold Brighouse, was considered good enough to have a place in the repertory of the National Theatre. To confirm the relevance of Miss Horniman, one need only add that Joan Littlewood's Theatre Workship was founded by a radical group in Manchester and that their first commercial success was Behan's *The Hostage*, a gaily subversive play in the O'Casey tradition.

Unless you can detect realism in playwrights like Pinero and similar practitioners of boulevard drama, which I can not, or consider Shaw a realist, which he was not, the influence of Ibsen on English realism was mainly academic. Was there a single dramatist in the English language who can be said to have digested Ibsen organically until Arthur Miller in the late nineteen-forties? It is true that the *Ghosts* production which so upset English critics in 1901 was put on by the gallant J. T. Grein, an admirer of Antoine's Théâtre Libre, and that Shaw's criticism immortalized the impact of Ibsen on the London commercial theatre. But the results there were marginal, mainly a loosening of restraints on boulevard drama and a sharpening of conventional situations, which lasted for half a century. Through two world wars and twenty years of insecurity between them, the gap between the London theatre and realities outside it was exceptionally continuous and deep. If realism means anything you would not expect to find it in 'the theatre of comfort'.

If, however, realism is a tendency latent in all drama, it will never be lost without trace. The links between Theatre Workshop and Miss Horniman prove that. So did the disturbance, now and then, of West End frivolity between the wars by Maugham, Sherriff and Mackenzie, all three of them reflecting post-war anxieties, but in the colourless, behaviourist idiom we call 'naturalistic'. To these gestures towards life outside the theatre one may add the continuous efforts of small, minority playhouses such as the Everyman and the Gate, which ensured a limited diffusion of Ibsen, Chekhov and Strindberg. But English writing remained derivative from, if not parasitic on, the great continentals until 1956 and the movement we associate with Osborne, Wesker, Arden and Pinter. In that year the centre of gravity of world drama shifted decisively to England. There was no riot at the first night of Osborne's *Look Back in Anger* and nothing in the play to compare with the mature rebelliousness of Synge and early O'Casey. There were, however, speeches denouncing the British military caste; there was an ironing board on stage; and there was the hero, a university graduate working at a sweet stall in a provincial market. To that extent *Look Back in Anger* was a move in the direction of realism, for none of those things would have been tolerated by a West End management. The play gave a theatrical voice to a new generation, otherwise it has little relevance to this subject. It has priority and topicality rather than importance.

Arden, Wesker and Pinter are another matter. One thing they have in common is a mastery of London or provincial working-class speech rhythms and dialect. It is important to stress the texture of the dialogue itself, because it is lost in translation. They select and manipulate it with conscious artifice, until it becomes a major factor in the dramatic effect, whereas before 1956 working-class dialect was confined to the urban variety theatres and to minor characters like the grotesque servants in West End plays. The range of serious drama is greatly increased when whole areas of regional speech are tapped in this way. It is no more 'realistic' than the speech of aristocratic comedy, but in English the popular dialects are notable not only for touches of archaic dignity but for colourful, concrete imagery. To name examples, the use of it by Wesker and Rudkin in plays about rural communities in Norfolk and Staffordshire is crucial, and at the same time untranslatable. In Delaney's *A Taste of Honey* it is the vitality of the Lancashire dialogue which distinguishes her work from that of Manchester School playwrights working on similar material in Miss Horniman's time. 'I write', Miss Delaney has said, 'as people speak.'

If we look at the mise-en-scène, the stage picture, and disregard the dialogue, the bias of these dramatists is evident. There is a stable, with soldiers lying on the floor alongside their equipment (Arden), a restaurant kitchen with its great ovens waiting to be heated, and another billet, this time at a training camp for airmen (both Wesker). There is a drab, untidy room with two iron beds (Pinter). The soldiers, the cooks and Pinter's destitute tramp are what you'd expect from a glance at the decor. They have nothing to do with Ibsen and Chekhov, but everything to do with Gorki. He, surely, like Synge, is a link with English realism of the nineteen-fifties. From Synge came its defiance of authority and respect for local dialect, from Gorki its cult of social outcasts in a grim setting. When *The Lower Depths* was produced by the Royal Shakespeare Company in 1962 a critic in *The Times* referred to 'the flood of realistic writing sprung from Gorki's example' and to the play's 'balance of aspiration and dusty fact'. Yet this, the first authoritative English production, took place no less than sixty years after the Moscow première. How, then, had Gorki's influence been exerted on the new English drama? The answer is, by way of the USA, aided by the possession of a common language. More precisely it was the realism of O'Neill and of the Method, both of them obviously more indebted to Gorki than to any other of the great realists of half a century before. We may narrow the process of infiltration still further, to a single production of *The Iceman Cometh* in 1958. This had an unexpected appeal to the young, and it was staged at the Arts, the same theatre as was later to show *The Lower Depths*.

If we look for the Russian masterpiece's 'balance of aspiration and dusty fact' in English work of the new dramatists, we find it often. Even the tramp in *The Caretaker*, a homeless wanderer like Luka, has aspirations of a kind. All will be well if he can reach a small town near London and find his identity papers. His host's mind is on a garden shed, which he thinks he is capable of building. Their surroundings are squalid, but the owner has dreams of transforming them by 'contemporary' decoration. In an interval of work in *The Kitchen*, five of the workers outline their ambitions. The equivalent of Satin is an emotional German cook, and the play builds up to the question 'What is there more?'. What more, that is, than the boredom, the violence and the squalor. It is their awareness of something beyond the dusty fact which raises the work of these dramatists above the mere documentation of ugliness.

The reasons for this long delayed impact of Gorki on the English theatre are complex and would repay entensive study. Obviously, however, they relate to the fact that the explosion of talent in 1956 was politically of the Left, whereas the commercial theatre had been overwhelmingly of the Right, as its neglect of Gorki, O'Casey and later of Brecht confirms. Two influences admitted by Wesker are those of O'Casey and Arthur Miller. Two plays, *The Entertainer* and *Serjeant Musgrave's Dance*, attacked Conservative foreign policy in, respectively, Suez and Cyprus. In so far as the Left's point of view, including the speech and sub-cultures of the working class, was no longer suppressed, this permitted an influx of subject-matter which brought the drama closer to life. Popular speech, a concern for the under-privileged and the dispossessed, a new freedom of political debate—all these combined towards realism. The long reign of boulevard drama was over. It was associated with Francophile dramatists and Francophile critics such as James Agate. The new movement rejected them and with them the 'naturalistic' conventions, the french windows and comic servants. The avant-garde work of Ionesco and Beckett, being rooted in fantasy, is irrelevant to Arden, Wesker and Littlewood. Even in Pinter it co-existed with English realism. If new forms were needed, they were looked for in Brecht and the English music-hall.

But the perennial source of English realism is in our literature, stretching from Chaucer to Dickens. To take a homely example, only what one may venture to call continental insularity could fail to notice the affinity of the mother in *A Taste of Honey* with Chaucer's Wife of Bath, a promiscuous hedonist with equally pungent speech, and both with the heroine of *La Celestina*, also produced by Miss Littlewood at Theatre Workshop. The drama's contact with life includes literature, especially a literature as rich and varied as the English. To return to our point of departure, Tom Robertson's *Caste* is palely but clearly Dickensian. One may add that this literary realism is diffused by the mass media, Dickens continually on television, Fielding in the film *Tom Jones*. But if we pretend, like some drama historians, that the progress of drama is confined to what happens in the theatre itself, there is a source which remains constant in England, even during a period such as the first half of the twentieth century when most new work was choked by convention. I mean Shakespeare, of course. Lukács has written of Shakespeare's 'refusal to weaken the popular liveliness of his scenes by any kind of "classicism"'. Now, half way through the nineteen-sixties, the vein of popular liveliness exploited by Wesker, Pinter and Littlewood shows signs of being exhausted. The English working class of the immediate post-war period no longer exists. For the moment, at any rate, the problems of success, leisure and a revolution in technology are more in the picture than the problems of the dispossessed. It is in the individual psyche that dramatists are searching for the lower depths. Meanwhile the drama lacks contact with politics and with science. Towards them, perhaps, it will make its next move in the direction of life, the next escape from its own conventions. Whatever happens realism will be active in the English theatre in its highest and, at the same time, most recognizable form. That is when Falstaff, the anti-hero, pauses on the battlefield to balance aspiration and dusty fact: 'What is Honour? . . . A word.'

During my boyhood in the nineteen-twenties we lived in a grim city of textile factories in the north of England. There was a very high incidence of rickets and other malnutrition diseases. In that city there was little or no sign of the Jazz Age we associate now with Noël Coward and Scott Fitzgerald, though one did hear of millowners' sons making bets with one another. It was rumoured that they would bet on who could spend a hundred pounds first during a week-end in London. It may have been left-wing propaganda, for that city was the birthplace of the Independent Labour Party. On the other hand, it may well have been true. Anything could happen in the nineteen-twenties. But for the majority life was dominated by slums, unemployment, pubs and association football. In the London West End theatre of the inter-war period there was a conspiracy of silence about these things. Shaw was permitted to discuss them in his plays, because he offered an oblique cerebral distillation of the concerns of the masses and never offended audiences with a direct view of the physical facts, the facts no one could miss who lived in an industrial city. Son of an alcoholic, Shaw was himself a fastidious puritan. His art shrinks from the symptoms of poverty, where that of Shakespeare did not. Instead of Poor Tom, the beggar in *King Lear*, instead of the human debris of the industrial revolution, Shaw won his London audiences with Alfred Doolittle, the comic dustman in *Pygmalion*, a music-hall caricature. It was another Irishman who broke the inter-war conspiracy of silence,

Sean O'Casey, and judging from the obituaries, many have not forgiven him yet. O'Casey, like Maxim Gorki and unlike Shaw, did not merely discuss urban degradation in the presence of well-fed theatre audiences, he showed it. Being a genius, he also humanized poverty by running up the dramatic scale of it from the ridiculous to the tragic, from Joxer in *Juno and the Paycock* to the heroine of the same play. I suppose his worst offence was not to have set the stage with a tenement instead of the customary luxurious drawing-room, but to have humanized the dispossessed occupants. Once poverty is humanized, as it is by Shakespeare, Gorki and O'Neill, as well as by O'Casey, we begin to see ourselves in it. Then it becomes difficult to endure, and for those who want the theatre to be a dream-factory, remote from life, impossible.

Born in a Dublin tenement himself. O'Casey depicted in his first three plays the anatomy of violence and squalor, without obscenity or any straining after adventitious or sadistic effect. The writer of his obituary in *The Times* believed that 'the spirit of the plays is far from being realistic. The Paycock, Joxer, Fluther and the Covey use language that was never spoken by mortal tenement dwellers'. And he refers them to a source in poetry, like Falstaff's. Quite apart from its revealing selection of comic characters only, I think this opinion disregards both the nature of realism and O'Caseys' dramatic method. Realism is not the exact reproduction of everyday language, nor is it confined to dialogue alone; it is the drama's tendency to reclaim areas of life excluded by the walls of convention. Realism is essentially subversive. In the case of Synge and of O'Casey it caused riots. As for Falstaff, the realism he embodies comes near to upsetting the hierarchy which it was Shakespeare's intention to uphold.

If we look to life, rather than 'a sea of poetry', for O'Casey's inspiration, it remains true that his dramatic method is a marriage of uncompromising realism with heightened speech. A model was ready to hand in Synge, a master of elaborate dialogue who wrote about peasants. O'Casey's originality lay in urbanizing the formula. Although he achieved the unlikely feat of adapting it to the life of the urban slums, the lower depths, that alone would not give us the right to call him great. He went further. He added to poetic squalor the crisis of war, and war in one of its extreme forms, where neighbours are divided and the threat is intimate. The abortive Easter Rising of 1916, of the Irish against the British, was not only a preview of later revolutions in Europe but a forcing house of O'Casey's art. As Yeats wrote, 'a terrible beauty is born'. Because they add this dimension to vivid war reporting, *Juno and the Paycock* and *The Plough and the Stars* are tragic. I count myself lucky to have seen them acted as such by the Abbey Players – Arthur Sinclair, Sara Allgood and Maire O'Neill – people with the experience of the Easter Rising in their bones. This was in the self-deluding nineteen-thirties, at remote suburban theatres on the fringe of London. Behind Joxer's comedy and Juno's fortitude and the colourful phrases lay the biblical message: 'man goeth to his long home and the mourners go about the streets'. At that time not only London, but I suspect most of Europe, did not want to hear it.

O'Casey had left Ireland, the source of his inspiration, in 1926. In my view, his subsequent plays are less important. But this opinion is subject to doubts shared by many critics about the expressionist elements in *The Silver Tassie, Within the Gates* and *Red Roses for Me*. An immediate duty of the English theatre is to give them the top-level production they have not received yet. Then we may know better. The usual opinion is to welcome O'Casey's expressionism as an artistic advance. I'm not so sure. I think it may be a formal evasion of his artistic dilemma. I do not think he was as fitted for exile as Joyce or Shaw. When the impulse stemming from the Easter Rising was exhausted, he adopted a European Marxist position, like Shaw and Brecht. And this position only leads to major drama when allied to an exceptional intellect. Having taught himself to read, heroically at the age of fourteen, O'Casey was too late a starter, perhaps, to make the adjustment.

On the other hand, his working-class origin, and apprentice-ship as a labourer rather than an intellectual, made him a culture hero of the new English dramatists of 1956. Worthy on his record of the highest official honours, here was a world-famous man of the theatre who, even in old age, made no concessions to established authority. True, his later plays can seem a decadent version of the Abbey Theatre tradition like the abuse of stage Irish on television. They leave an impression of frustrated genius in search of a better subject. But they glorify youth and sex. They are, as O'Casey himself was, always on the side of life. You can read his influence most obviously, of course, in *The Quare Fellow* and *The Hostage* by Brendan Behan. But O'Casey's influence goes much further than that. It extends to Arden, Wesker, Delaney, Rudkin, Alun Owen and a dozen others, wherever in fact urban dialect is shaped, selected and built up to the purposes of serious drama, wherever the rejects of society, the soldiers in *Serjeant Musgrave's Dance* or the rustics in *Afore Night Come*, are put in the centre of the stage and given a voice. They copied his faults, too, whenever they cultivated a folksy togetherness or let feeble stereotypes put the case for the ruling classes. From 1956 onwards the theatres of the West End itself resounded with the harsh, repetitive, but often poetic rhythms of popular speech. These playwrights had utterly destroyed the commercial theatre's conspiracy of silence, and if O'Casey wanted revenge for his neglect, this was it.

I think he knew that only Eugene O'Neill excelled him in our time as a dramatist in the English language. In verbal agility and colour O'Casey had the advantage, but at his best he did not depend on the lilt of an Irish voice. At the climax of *The Plough and the Stars* an English corporal enters the tenement and orders the removal of a coffin. It contains the body of a girl who has died of tuberculosis during the Easter Rising. The corporal has no time for ceremony, He is facing death himself, from snipers in the streets. Tragedy has gone beyond words here; it lies in the irony of the situation. All previous dramatists from Shakespeare onwards who have achieved this terrible, compassionate irony, even once or twice, are now regarded as permanent members of the living theatre.

At the end of *Mourning Becomes Electra* the heroine announces that she has chosen to go on living. Her mother and her brother have both committed suicide during the course of the trilogy. 'That's escaping punishment,' says Lavinia. 'And there's no one left to punish me. I'm the last Mannon. I've got to punish myself.' She orders the gardener to nail up the windows and then goes into the house. . . . In 1937 an acquaintance of mine went to see *Mourning Becomes Electra* at the Westminster Theatre. When he got home he killed himself by carbon monoxide. The text had been available for three years in England, and for all I know the unhappy man may have been familiar with it. But nobody is likely to be deeply affected merely by reading O'Neill. The test is what he does to you in the theatre, in public, as for instance a quarter of a century later when audiences had become short-winded listeners compared with those of 1937. Yet *The Iceman Cometh* took a hold of people at the Arts Theatre for three and a quarter hours. In neither play is there any compromise with the supposed limitations of theatre audiences. In neither is there a gracefully turned sentence or a final glimmer of hope. They deal in defeat.

Before trying to justify O'Neill as a playwright, it's important to underline his curious relevance to today's impulses in the drama. I say curious, because he cuts a rather musclebound ponderous figure on stage, a very long way from the hipster's rhythm, which tends to be feline, mercurial, off-beat. Compare

The Iceman Cometh with another group of pipe-dreamers in Gelber's *The Connection* or for that matter, compare O'Neill with his opposite in American literature, Scott Fitzgerald. In other ways O'Neill's climate of drama is one we share. There's the preoccupation with masks and problems of identity, with clumsy gestures of personal communication across a void, with man reduced to animal responses. There's the use of lengthy monologues, and there's drama extracted, as far back as *All God's Chillun* of 1923, from oppressive enclosure in a room. All these are characteristic of the mid-century avant-garde. Nowadays, if anyone killed himself after a performance, it would be regarded as a significant action in the tradition of Albert Camus. Alongside its affinities with the avant-garde, O'Neill's drama takes in a lot of the territory we link with social realism. It excels in dealing with the underprivileged, with outcasts lovingly brought to life in the vernacular. The first set of equipment is a legacy from Strindberg, acknowledged as his master when O'Neill won the Nobel prize. The other is from Maxim Gorki. Either of them could be, and in fact have been, put to use on drama at a conscious level of studying literary models, but not with full conviction. Reading the vast biography of O'Neill by Arthur and Barbara Gelb, we are left in no doubt at all that both these usually separated influences went down to the roots of O'Neill's personality. A man whose brother could say, 'I made sin easy for him' was tuned in early on Strindberg's emotional wavelength. As for squalor, O'Neill was able to boast of one of his drinking haunts, 'Gorki's *Lower Depths* was an ice-cream parlour by comparison'.

Some of O'Neill's work, then, gets across in today's theatre. He was also the pipeline between that theatre and two of its dominant influences from the past, Gorki and Strindberg. In addition, his affinity with them went further than conscious admiration. It was also a matter of temperament and experience. What else is relevant on our way to placing him? Obviously, that he was American. Among other things, the Gelbs's biography covers a hundred years of social history. At the age of eighteen O'Neill is opting out of the American way of life and consorting with, for example, One Lung Curran, who drinks wood alcohol flavoured with Worcester sauce. But before the end he is preening himself in a mink-lined overcoat, bought from Broadway success. A lot could be made of this contrast and of his dogged refusal of political commitment. A lot could also be made of his influence on American dramatists like Arthur Miller and Tennessee Williams, not to mention our own New Wave, notably Arnold Wesker, and of course the Method. One wonders whether a minor dramatist has ever held so central a position in the drama of his time, whether a minor dramatist could fill nine hundred and seventy pages of the Gelbs's biography with such a distinct, though not very attractive, personality. But none of this amounts to an evaluation, and the claim I make for O'Neill is that, so far and at his best, he is the greatest dramatist to have written in the English language in the twentieth century.

The paradox is that he couldn't write, the way Balzac and frequently Dickens, and often enough Conrad and even at times Faulkner, couldn't write. Only with O'Neill it was all the time. Consider this: 'Darkness without a star to guide us! Where are we going, Vinnie? Oh, I know you think you know where, but there's many a slip, remember!' That is from *Mourning Becomes Electra*, Part Three, Act Two, one of the high points of his art; and it is a fair sample of his prose. But when I heard Beatrix Lehmann utter those words in 1937, and Barbara Jefford again at the Old Vic in 1961, I was in no condition to analyse the prose. It just didn't seem to matter. At the Old Vic I talked in the interval with a classics graduate who is also one of our most promising directors. It didn't seem to matter to him, either. Nor does it matter to Katina Paxinou, who pioneered O'Neill in Greece back in the nineteen-thirties. The conclusion is that O'Neill's prose transmits something beyond its intrinsic value. In the case of *Mourning Becomes Electra*, what it transmits is Dionysian energy, and beyond that the New England tradition of Hawthorne, grafted precisely on an Aeschylean framework.

I regard O'Neill's competitors for pre-eminence in his time as Shaw, Synge and O'Casey: all Irishmen, of whom O'Neill is the only one whose dramatic writing lacks charm. But what use is charm on the outside limits of human experience? O'Neill's concern for extremes took him from the disintegration of personality (*The Hairy Ape*) to the last word in assertiveness, Lavinia standing in for God.

5. SHAKESPEARE

The Actor and the Text

For the nineteen-sixties the scope of this subject is determined by two events: by the ending of the Old Vic's tenancy of the New Theatre in 1949 and by the setting up of the National Theatre in 1963. The first brought to an end the partnership of two great actors, Olivier and Richardson, working under favourable conditions not found again until the summer of 1962 when Olivier conducted his own season at Chichester. The second event amounted to an underwriting of those conditions by the Government and the London County Council. Essentially the conditions are a product of subsidy, repertory and a concentration of artistic forces. At the start of the period they also applied to the Gielgud-Ashcroft seasons at the Haymarket and at the close of it to the Royal Shakespeare's expansion. Although these were initially private ventures, attached to Littler and the Tennent organization, the assumption behind them was the same. The classics, including Shakespeare, can no longer be expected to pay for themselves.

It may seem a long way from these complex issues of finance to the critical appreciation of Shakespearian acting. That task might seem to begin at the moment the first lines are spoken and the audience settles down. For inter-war critics it effectively did. There would be actors on view who were known to have served their apprenticeship with Tree, Benson or Granville-Barker; innovations took place against a reasonably stable background. They could be identified readily and defined at length. James

Agate, for example, had space enough to tell you what Benson had done with a passage in *Richard II* before reporting on a newcomer to the part. He also applied specific tests of skill, one of which was Othello's reaction to the drunken brawl:

> *Cassio, I love thee;*
> *But never more be officer of mine . . .*
> *Look if my gentle love be not rais'd up.*
> *I'll make thee an example.*

> *(II, iii)*

One can think of few critics more remote than Agate from the close-analysis school, yet here he was in touch with it, equally aware of the changes of tone and emotion in the passage quoted. Apart from the pounding severity of the second line, it is not remarkable as verse. Its quality is in the interplay of Othello's feelings, worn on his sleeve as usual and manipulated by Iago, who has staged the entire incident like an expert author directing his own work. Method acting, incapable of rhetoric or sublimity, would be quite in place here, not only for Othello, but for Iago and Cassio, too. But how can useful criticism of such an episode come about if there is no room to quote? Ban quotation, either for reasons of space or in deference to a journalistic fashion for jaunty writing, and you discard the main point of reference, the true focus of judgment, the text. From there it is a short step to favouring sets, costumes, or the director's 'ruling idea', factors more easily dealt with in a brief report. Where Agate's point of reference was Shakespeare's words, interpreted by the latest of a line of actors lodged in the memory for comparison, the reality of post-war dramatic criticism is often a journalist besieging the theatre's press officer in order to find out why *Much Ado about Nothing* has been dressed for the early nineteenth century. At its crudest this approach is summed up by a hasty question in the first interval: 'What's the gimmick?' Long before the first lines are spoken and while the audience is filing in, the gimmick may already have announced itself from the uncurtained set. It may well take three hours to decide on its merits and these may distract attention from nuances of acting, like the cordite in *Henry V in*

Battledress (Mermaid, 1960). Nor will the actors have a training background as narrowly Shakespearian as that of the Bensonians. James Booth, the Royal Shakespeare Edmund of 1962, was dressed in tight trousers resembling jeans. His best-known performances had been as a Soho spiv and an RAF cook.

'I am resentful if criticism is uninformed or dismissive,' Peter Hall has said. 'After all, it is the only record of our work.' During the period under survey it has been a hasty and superficial record. Shakespearian acting has thus been deprived of one of its most valuable encouragements and supports. So much, that one has to remind oneself what its function is. It is to perform Shakespeare's plays in the medium they were written for, that is, live theatre, not films, television, radio or on disc, though all these substitutes have their uses. Parts like Hamlet, Antony, Cleopatra, Macbeth, Othello and Falstaff demand a range of expression rarely to be found in any one person. They are so exacting that the history of great interpreters is a history of incomplete successes, yet even partial success can illuminate the plays in a manner unknown to study of the written words. And in addition to the heroic central figures, the plays require large casts, the least of whom may find himself given a line of major poetry. To build a company of strength enough to satisfy both the major and minor acting demands would take more time and money than has ever been spent on the performing of Shakespeare in England. The business of star actors is to embody the Hamlets, Antonys and Othellos and to convey the magnificent language assigned them; the business of the others is to understand and further the grand design of each play. This unity of solo work and ensemble, this collective expression of riches obvious in the text, demands a concentration of artistic forces.

Under the pressure of war a hint of the ideal concentration was given by the New and Haymarket seasons. Gielgud, Olivier, Redgrave, Evans, Ashcroft, and Richardson were seen to be the greatest collection of Shakespearian actors within living memory. Then, after a few years of peace, dispersal began. With the rocketing of West End land values, speculators evicted the artists unless their terms were met, and their terms were the bad old inter-war terms, worst of all the long run, the relentless squeezing of profit from a success. Another was the toleration of Shakespeare under the imprint of star names on a budget too low for proper casting of other parts. A third was the assemblage and dismissal of *ad hoc* companies, to the detriment of group acting. Yet a fourth, scarcely noticed, was the promiscuous camping in different theatre buildings, none of which had time to acquire Shakespearian identity as the New had managed to do. Between 1946 and 1953 *Antony and Cleopatra* was produced at the Piccadilly, the Prince's and the St James's. One result of the haphazard muddling through was the exclusion of great performances from the capital city. Gielgud's Angelo, Redgrave's Lear and Olivier's Macbeth had one thing in common; either you made the journey to Stratford-on-Avon or you never saw them at all.

The stars met this reactionary threat to their wartime glory by compromising with a situation loaded in favour of the speculator. They could earn enough money on the films or in entertainment pieces to force Shakespeare into the West End from time to time, into such theatres as were not held by long-running musicals, thrillers or farces. They could insist on limited runs, but no longer on repertory, supposedly disliked by the public, though it had filled the New and the Haymarket a few years before and was accepted eagerly for opera and the ballet. What they could not achieve was continuity, a secure foothold and a permanent company. None of them could afford to buy or build a theatre, and without that all efforts to stabilize the situation were doomed. The artistic needs of great actors, the cultural needs of a newly educated public, the country's prestige, as well as any duty owed to Shakespeare himself, all came lower in the scale of priorities than the profits to be milked from a few square feet of land in Central London. Symptomatic of this blinkered materialism was the reluctance of successive governments to disgorge the money earmarked for the National Theatre. We are dealing with cultural, not political priorities, it should be emphasized. Attempts were repeatedly made to defend the fitful and half-hearted commercial exploitation of Shakespeare. First, by pointing to achievements like Gielgud's Benedick, Ashcroft's Beatrice and Olivier's Titus, all mounted outside London originally. In relation to the talent existing, these were mere glimpses. Second in justification was the vicious fallacy, so convenient to speculators, that actors are rogues and vagabonds who wilt in security. This argument, which makes sense to a cynical employer exploiting a surplus of labour, lost its teeth when applied to titled actors of world renown. It acted as a brake on progress, however, especially when allied to another fallacy which seeks to deny actors any skill in practical affairs.

Such degrading philistinism in an age of affluence was peculiar to England and in England peculiar to the drama, Shakespeare included. It did not apply to opera and the ballet, both munificently subsidized. One day the causes may be traced, perhaps discovered as far back as the closing of the theatres in 1642. Its effect on the acting of Shakespeare in the nineteen-fifties was simple. Great acting was rationed when an unprecedented number of admittedly great actors were in their prime. To cite homely examples, which most people interested in the subject can parallel, I was abroad on active service at the time of Richardson's Falstaff (New, 1945). I have still not seen it, because it has not been repeated, not once in twenty years, though it is widely claimed to be the best of our time. Nor have I seen the growth of Olivier's Macbeth since the version he did under Saint-Denis (New, 1937), later perfected but never shown to London, not even as a film, for the projected Rank Organization production was shelved. Such are the results when definitive performances are at the mercy of the open market. To deny the goodwill and public spirit of all commercial managements would be unjust, but the record of omissions speaks for itself. It is as if key masterpieces in the National Gallery were withdrawn from circulation for years at a time, with this grim difference, that actors age quicker than paintings and cannot be restored. The most they can expect is preservation on film. Hence the importance of a system which keeps their best work in regular circulation.

Such a system has long been perfected abroad, on the foundations of subsidy, repertory and concentration of force. The fruits of it were demonstrated in London by the Comédie Française,

the Moscow Art Theatre and the Berliner Ensemble. They confirmed the excellence of our Shakespearian star actors and no
visiting actor improved on them. The visitors' superiority lay in
teamwork and a pleasantly arrogant self-confidence reaching to
the smallest parts. Everybody seemed to know exactly what they
were about. The lesson was not lost on English actors. In 1957
Gielgud said that he envied the foreign companies their possession
of a particular theatre building and ability to build up a stable
repertory. That an actor of his eminence and achievement could
take this attitude is of great significance. At the time he was playing in one of Noël Coward's less inspired comedies and he was
soon to tour Shakespeare alone, in recitals. In neither role was he
in the true relationship of a star Shakespearian actor to other
actors and the public, scaling the heights of his art in a way to be
remembered by the company on stage with him and the people
in front. The likely conclusion is that adverse conditions had
forced him out of circulation.

Other alternatives to improvised West End Shakespeare were
offered by the expansion of air travel and a reservoir of audiences
in, for example, Canada and the United States. This led to valuable pioneering, but increased the dispersal of talent. Another
centrifugal influence was the attraction of television, aggravated
by yet one more, the new pattern of filming on location abroad.
The situation was summed up by an article in *The Times* of
27th February 1959, headed 'How we Waste our Best Actors'.
'There is plenty of labour being done, but exactly how far creative
energy can be spread across different media and hemispheres
without loss of quality is not yet known.' On 16th January 1962
another article in the same paper gave an answer. 'The past year',
it began, 'has been unsatisfactory in a branch of drama which the
English might be expected to excel in – that is, the performing of
Shakespeare.' And the heading was 'What is the Remedy for Bad
Shakespearian Acting?' By that time the consequences of dispersal were becoming obvious. It had created a gap in the tradition of Shakespearian acting. Why had this not been filled by
the Old Vic, back in Waterloo Road, and the Memorial Theatre
at Stratford-on-Avon? Because neither could hold a company

together long enough to consolidate. Casting had become a nightmare of detection, of tracking down actors in a network of airports, film and television studios, of co-ordinating engagements in several different media. The city of Bradford, where Irving had died in 1905, saw no professional Shakespeare for a decade.

The gap was filled by directors, mostly wandering freelances like the actors and subject to the same distractions. With the example of Shakespearian stars absent, as it usually was, the younger directors and actors had to grope towards the most exacting plays in the language as best they could. The environment they shared was dominated by moving pictures, American Method acting and the English New Wave drama of 1956 onwards. Many things in the Shakespearian repertoire will yield to an approach on these lines, but they are no guide to aristocratic behaviour or the delivery of lyrical and rhetorical verse. One would have thought a suitable style could have been arrived at from a study of the text. However, it turned out otherwise, and it is only fair to add that younger French actors of the same period were known to mangle Racine just as badly. Regrettably, though, this deficiency was rarely admitted and the results were passed off as a valid recreation of the plays in modern terms. In fact they were an evasive distortion, masking incompetence.

One of innumerable examples was the Old Vic's rendering of *King John*, III. i., where Constance laments her son and curses his murderers. This scene, one of the high points of Shakespeare's art, fell flat, and so, literally, did Maxine Audley, on the stage floor in spasms of grief. There are two points to note. On the first night, at any rate, several of her lines were inaudible. This is excusable in Method acting of plays in which the context may matter more than the lines as written, but Constance's lines in this scene were obviously written with care, if not inspiration, and the verse was clearly intended to bear the main weight of the action. Secondly, Miss Audley is a talented Shakespearian actress with full command of Shakespearian verse, as she proved in *Titus Andronicus* (1957) at the Stoll Theatre (capacity 2,400) where she was more audible than Olivier himself. For her Constance fiasco the blame must lie on the director, Peter Potter, whether the approach was her idea or his. It is evident at a glance that the episode will not yield to Method acting, unlike the *Othello* passage already quoted. Another mystery was Miss Audley's disappointing Lady Macbeth. Or rather it would be a mystery, but for the connection I have indicated between acted Shakespeare and conditions working against it. Here was a beautiful actress with all the relevant experience, including Third Programme radio leads, fatal women in popular thrillers and Emilia to Orson Welles's Othello. Correctly applied, it must have added up to a splendid Lady Macbeth.

The waste of talent exemplified by Miss Audley's Old Vic appearances was echoed for an older generation by Wolfit's banishment to recitals, for a younger, by O'Toole's defection to films after a single season at Stratford-on-Avon. How far this waste was the fault of the actors concerned is not the point. The logic of the situation had become inescapable. A decade of Shakespearian acting talent ranging in age and style from Gielgud's Lear to O'Toole's Hamlet had failed to produce any revival comparable with the all-round standards of Glyndebourne and the Royal Ballet. Mozart had been better mounted than Shakespeare; Verdi's *Othello* had been better mounted than Shakespeare's; and on the international touring circuit, Chekhov and Brecht. The exceptional crop of stars, old and new, tended to mask the truth by improvised successes. But actors and directors new to Shakespeare inherited chaos. The truth was that the institutions formerly entrusted with the nurture of Shakespearian acting no longer sufficed. They had to be replaced.

Models for the new institutions were to hand. Essentially they conformed to Granville-Barker's blueprint for an exemplary theatre. The New and Haymarket seasons, the foreign visitors, the example of the ballet, had struck roots in England. Just in time, when shoddy presentation was in danger of classing Shakespeare as a bore, an archaic survival to be smuggled under a disguise of gimmicks, the means of presentation began to come under the control of those best fitted to understand them, the artists themselves. Olivier became director of the National Theatre, Brook and Saint-Denis directors of the Royal Shakespeare along with Peter Hall, who had extended the system of repertory and a permanent company from Stratford to the West End itself. John Neville, one of the best recent products of the defunct Old Vic, was appointed a co-director of the new civic theatre at Nottingham. In 1963 the way seemed clear for a concentration of forces in the best interests of Shakespearian acting. The battle had been won, at a price. By 1963, O'Toole and Finney, both on the brink of greatness, had not acted in Shakespeare for more than two years, Richard Burton for longer still. Some of the great actors and actresses were past their best. Spurious reputations, premature and dubious successes, had been won. Critical standards had fallen, because digestion adapts itself to a mediocre diet.

It would have been pleasanter to drape this study round a collection of jewelled performances, but that would have been to accept haphazard, hit-or-miss, attempts at what should be systematic. The roles of Hamlet and Macbeth should not be hawked around a competitive economy until the right man condescends to fit them in between a musical comedy and a film. They are a privilege, to be accepted in secure surroundings and enjoyed with humility. The proper conditions and atmosphere are now in sight. The artistic problems remain, and the worst of them spring from the absence of any recognized school of Shakespearian acting during the period, any blending of innovation and continuity.

Much could be learnt from an organization which grew up outside the focal points of contention, the National Youth Theatre. It was improvised by Michael Croft, a master at Alleyn's School, but on the sound principles of meaningful grouping, well drilled crowds and virile, eloquent speech. The company matured together, some of them through university and drama school, without dispersing until 1962 when the eldest were absorbed by professional drama and other careers. By that time the founder members had become the only Shakespearian ensemble in England and it would have been in the national interest to hold them together at any price. They had been well received in the West End and in Paris. Gielgud, Guinness, Redgrave, Byam

Shaw, Hall and Neville were on their council, with Richardson as president. But in the lean, declining years of the Old Vic, Croft was never invited to direct there, nor at Stratford-on-Avon. It was as if those in charge of Shakespeare's theatrical headquarters had little confidence in a director committed first and foremost to Shakespeare's text.

Father Figure

'What made Shakespeare possible was that Lord Lucas called on the Barkers one morning to say that he had sold his pig-farm.' Thus Harley Granville-Barker's biographer, C. B. Purdom, begins his account of the 1912 Savoy productions of *The Winter's Tale* and *Twelfth Night*, generally agreed to have been among the most complete artistic successes known in the modern theatre. It has taken forty years to modify the philistinism which could leave the fate of our leading dramatist to an aristocratic whim or to the missionary zeal of a fanatical do-gooder like Lilian Baylis. Barker's advocacy of a National Theatre as early as 1907 already rejected the haphazard subsidy he was condemned to put up with himself; and what he thought of the other solution can be gathered from a reference in 1940 to 'that dreadful Old Vic'. As neither a folk-theatre nor a West End gamble would satisfy him, the logic of the situation forced him out of the theatre in his prime.

It would be easy to interpret this withdrawal as the act of a heartless perfectionist, unfit for the rough traffic of the drama, or as the retreat of a febrile romantic, Shaw's original Marchbanks, from the crack-up of the First World War. As an actor of the pre-cinema era he fades into the limbo of written reports and quaint Edwardian stills. As a playwright, in spite of Miss Margery Morgan's patient advocacy, he is stuck with ponderous domesticity in the 'well-made' convention. His play *Waste*, it is true, deals with the sexual lapse of a politician. Its reticence, however, has fallen a long way behind the march of events and the central issue of Church Disestablishment has grown to seem parochial. Barker's fastidiousness would be enough to set him aside from the social and political upheavals of the inter-war years. Having offended the interests vested in drama as a commercial speculation, and with his part in the Royal Court seasons of Shaw and Galsworthy, he might have found an affinity with leftish protest. O'Casey and Odets are incongruous companions to think up for him, even satirically. The image, instead, is one of studious affluence, a second prosperous marriage and academic work in the United States, of someone on another planet from, say, Dylan Thomas. Although the causes and course of Barker's 'defection' await a study which would throw light on pre-war London far beyond the concerns of drama, he resists canonization as a rebel. Archetypal outsiders do not end as director of the British Institute in Paris. To put it mildly, his was not a career to inflame imagination in the nineteen-sixties. Nevertheless, the theatre's logistics come closer every year to those he set out; and his withdrawal from an active part in its affairs was a myth. First, among some of his best successors his word has remained law to this day. Second, Barker developed a genius for directing Shakespeare on paper.

The importance of his *Prefaces to Shakespeare*, now reprinted in a paperback edition with foreword, illustrations and notes by M. St Clare Byrne, is not to be gauged without bearing in mind the tenacity of Barker's influence backstage. Since the director's control of production forces him unavoidably into the role of a *de facto* critic and Barker's *Prefaces* are written appraisals, he is as accident-prone as any other writer who systematically confronts the passionate complexity of Shakespeare's work and tries to make his own limited sense of it. Mr Purdom condemns Barker's adherence to the A. C. Bradley emphasis on drama as a conflict of character, though without putting forward anything less arguable himself. Not only is controlling imagery an absentee from the *Prefaces*, but the epic continuity now found in the Roman plays is unsuspected; *Julius Caesar* is no more than a dummy run on the way to tragedy. Nor is there any precise historical hindsight of the kind which can view Caesar's assassination as regicide, anathema to Tudor audiences, or can spot the gentlemanly scruples which are the ruin of Shakespearian heroes confronted with *realpolitik*. Iago is only 'Machiavellian' in inverted commas. Sensuality is denied to Desdemona and, even in her 'Gallop apace' outburst, to Juliet. Behind the decorum thought to have been imposed by the original boy actors there is a well-bred recoil from much of life and, for that matter, of the plays. So one might go on, reconstructing the starchy hero of *Waste* in juxtaposition to mercurial Elizabethans. It would be a useful exercise in criticism and it would miss the point, which is that Barker's *Prefaces* are a bridge between the Shakespearian text and the public.

Of these twin pillars of his reputation, the stagecraft and the scholarship, the former is not easy to pin down. Busy theatre people are under no obligation to log the course of their ideas. Moreover, in the inter-war period when Barker's influence was decisive, English actors and directors were still inhibited by an insular 'showbiz' mystique from public discussion of the technical and artistic sides of their work. To the researcher they might have been conjurers unwilling to betray an illusion. If, for example, one looked to Noël Coward's autobiography for help in the tone and timing of comedy, the result was a blank. Yet all this time the staging of Shakespeare was steadily maturing to the harvest of the great New and Haymarket seasons towards the end of the Second World War. The process can now be seen to have had the subtle coherence of organic growth. As always with the drama, it depended very much on the interplay of personalities. People with backgrounds and temperaments as far apart as Richardson and Saint-Denis had a place in it. Looked at as a whole, it had a variety and vitality not too far short of the almost impossible demands made by the plays themselves. That it really was a movement we can now tell, after several years of discontinuity and confusion of aim in the staging of classical revivals. Was it just a lucky pile-up of talent, or was there a binding agent? Certainly there was no 'ruling idea'. English empiricism, the professional evasiveness already mentioned, perhaps the danger Shaw wisely avoided, of seeming to take the drama seriously, prevented that. The ideal authority, if you aimed at artistic standards in the commercial frivolity of the inter-war theatre, would be an admired absentee, an oracle who could be relied on not to offend the speculators or the do-gooders who footed the bill by being actually seen to intrude. This *éminence grise* was Granville-Barker.

To sustain such a view of his place in the scheme one might rely on the prestige of his revolutionary Savoy productions of 1912, kept alive in the memories of those who took part in them; but Lillah McCarthy's account written twenty years later is a warning against that line of argument. The director's first wife and leading lady in the productions, she describes them scrappily. We learn that the first of them failed to attract the public and come up with a thud against Edmund Gosse's opinion that the Leontes was 'quite a feat of memory'. Although such chat is frustrating, it fits well enough with the title, *Myself and my Friends*, and those at the heart of a great dramatic event are not expected to be its historians. Fortunately there is firmer evidence of Barker's authority. It runs from 1929 to 1940, looped round three key men in the history of Shakespearian staging, all of them directors and one a great actor as well. In 1929, Harcourt Williams took over at the Old Vic. 'Harley Granville-Barker', he writes, 'was the one man I was determined to talk to before I plunged into the actual work of the season. He had just published his first volume of *Prefaces to Shakespeare. . . .*' Guthrie, his successor at the Old Vic four years later, had also read the *Prefaces* and intended to follow 'Poel and Barker and Shaw'. Finally Gielgud, who had blossomed under the direction of Williams, with all the reliance on Barker which that implies, went to the fountain head. In 1940 he rehearsed *King Lear* under the direction of Barker himself.

What exactly were the principles of production which could dominate a great age of Shakespearian staging by remote control? Briefly, they rested on a functional equivalent of what Miss Byrne, in her exemplary foreword to the present edition, calls the 'austere replica of the Globe' used by his master, Poel. A forestage was thrust out over the orchestra pit, lights were banked in front of the circle. Any scenic illusion inside the proscenium arch came strictly second to what the actors did and said. They could flaunt themselves and their costume, free from the grandiose and unwieldly sets we saw an example of in Zeffirelli's *Othello*. It was Barker's belief that in high points of drama we ought scarcely to be aware of the set. Irksome scene changing, copious cutting and ham diction were out; continuity and a briskly taken full text were in. The objective, later invoked to justify grotesquely ill-reformed gimmicks – including relapses into Victorian clutter – was to bring Shakespeare alive to modern audiences. It was well done again and again, by others working more or less to Barker's plan. Where there were failures, in what after all can be thought of as a routine matter of national prestige, the defect can nearly always be traced to the same cause: too much concern for the audience and too little for Shakespeare. It leads above all to a lack of confidence in the text, to mistrust of its holding-power without visual aids and to neurotic anxiety about the right way to speak it. Barker, on the other hand, saw the text as a weapon, and on the evidence of the *Prefaces* he knew more about it than any other director.

Was his scholarship any more than secondary, a siphoning off of other men's work, of value only where it led to literate staging? It would be rash to assume that it was. For many years there has been a shifting of the centre of gravity in drama studies, parallel with an increase of separate university departments equipped with theatres, towards research on the plays in action. This makes for disruption of ingrained academic habit. Although much has been found out by private reading of works conditioned by the need for getting across to a theatre public, that approach can be faulted on the grounds that the primary source is not a script, no matter how fine the writing, but a performance. One may be struck by the length of time scholars had been at work on the plays before Professor Empson pointed out the function of the double plot, as the interaction of two important devices and not just a means of letting cheerfulness break in. Reading offers leisure to bother about matters of time and place, when the public is concerned with neither and a skilful dramatist has allowed for the fact. Barker's practical experience left him immune to pedantic irrelevancies and gave him a sharp eye for what was likely to be going on between the lines. He notices the distribution of lines in a way only possible to one who knows what it means to actors. Hence: 'The simplest reason for Juliet's leave-taking of life being short is that Romeo's has been long.' He stresses the overriding importance of Shakespeare's alternation of scenes. Perhaps his greatest achievement was to visualize the plays in action, in terms of Tudor conditions where these have a bearing on the structure. No other critic conveys the feeling of sitting next to the dramatist at rehearsal.

Since Barker's death in 1946 and the delay in forming a National Theatre, in which his influence could have been kept fresh, tested and in part handed on, revivals of Shakespeare have been erratic and at times atrocious. Young actors and directors, having no consistent authority at home, formed their ideas from Stanislavsky, the Method and Brecht, none of them at all definitive in the staging of Shakespeare. There was a confused search for 'style', based very properly on envy of the way foreign actors of Chekhov, Brecht and Molière have an air of knowing precisely what they are about. But by the time Kazan admitted that the Method did not hold the key to formal diction, blank verse had taken a severe beating from actors forcing a shaggy virility into lyrical passages or filtering its groundswell through subjective 'inner feeling'. The director's ruling idea could range from a prissy romanticism to anachronistic Marxist glosses. It was left to Stella Adler, a pioneer of American realism, to point out that 'the circumstances of Hamlet are in Elsinore, in the fact that he is a Renaissance man, not modern man'.

This decline took place when the Sidgwick and Jackson edition of the *Prefaces* was hard to come by. Its successor, the Batsford illustrated one, costs four guineas. So it cannot be said that the *Prefaces* have been readily available to young people travelling light. If they had been we would surely have had a less tentative approach to the plays and fewer solecisms in performance. As it is, a generation at least as gifted as the one before has grown up almost in ignorance of a major source of inspiration and down-to-earth help. On this assumption the paperback volumes are buttressed by pictures and notes which amount to a concise production history of each play concerned. Miss Byrne has made of them a valuable contribution in their own right.

What will today's theatre people think of the *Prefaces*? Is Barker's influence due for embalming or resurrection? Gielgud's acting has become something of a minority taste, or seemed to have before his recent Joseph Surface. Not everyone will thrill to be reminded that his *Lear* passage in *The Ages of Man* is set in the mould Barker directed. Nor is the *Othello* preface the best of competitors with Stanislavsky's blueprint, especially in its patrician contempt for Iago. Barker, with his subtle genius for giving offence, sees Iago's personality as that of an actor. But it may surprise newcomers to discover how closely the *Romeo and Juliet* preface fits the ruling idea of Zeffirelli's outstandingly popular version and to learn that the 1912 Savoy productions were staged in a clear, surgical light, in fact a Brechtian light. There was even a grapple with epic drama: *The Dynasts*, on a bare stage with the commentator. To put that on in the mood of November 1914 was the reverse of escapist.

On the Screen

'I have one principle,' said Ingmar Bergman in an interview for *The Times*, 'what is in the text. . . . To make clear to the audience what the writer has meant. To lose the text in spectacle? I think that is terrible. The principle is the same for *The Merry Widow* or *Macbeth*.' There Bergman was speaking as a man of the theatre, in reference to the medium for which *Macbeth* and *The Merry Widow* were conceived. But he is better known as a film director, and like all the great ones with the exception of Orson Welles, Bergman has never made a film of Shakespeare. It is easy to see why. He wants to create, rather than be a junior partner, an interpreter of something already overwhelmingly good. So the great film makers – Chaplin, Cocteau, Bergman, Visconti – write their own scripts, or exercise full control over the scriptwriter. And even in partnership with an eminent living writer, a personal style is evolved, the director's style, his own recognizable fusion of sound and image. The danger of losing a text in spectacle doesn't arise, because a film script remains a blueprint for what goes on in the studio. It serves the camera, and its existence is shadowy and provisional until it has been transferred to the screen by the director, by which time it has something else. On the other hand, the text of poetic drama has a tough, independent existence. The better it is, the less it needs illustration. What you get in the best films is a director's personal style, and the better that is, the less it has to gain from fidelity to, or more likely competition with, the personal style of Shakespeare or any other poetic dramatist. This may explain why the best films using Shakespeare's own words have been made by directors of the second rank: Olivier, Mankiewicz and Castellani.

What I mean by directors of the second rank are those with something less than a compulsive urge to create in terms of the screen, and they might even include Orson Welles at the time he made *Macbeth* and *Othello*. For a good compromise between the needs of Shakespeare and the needs of the screen, the three Olivier films are in a class by themselves, because they respect both the text and the camera. The only vulgarizations they contain are the guying of the two prelates who outline Henry's claim to the French throne, and the notorious description of Hamlet as a man who could not make up his mind. Otherwise you feel an interesting tension between the cinema and the original plays. An obvious problem is the soliloquies, for conniving with the audience is easier in the theatre. The first solution was to hold Olivier's face in close-up, not seen to be speaking, with the words on sound-track, an idea presumably taken over from MGM's film of O'Neill's *Strange Interlude*. This is not entirely a happy device, perhaps because the effect of it can be self-consciously arty, as if drawing attention to a clever thing the medium can do. At all events, it is discarded in *Richard III*, where Olivier's direct address to the audience builds up a jaunty complicity, often funny, and at the same time disconcerting, in view of the enormity of Richard's behaviour. Here the supposed intimacy of the theatrical soliloquy, which really involves a good deal of conventional artifice and projection, gives way to a casual, throwaway delivery, such as can only be picked up by the microphone and the camera in close-up. In theatrical terms the soliloquy and the aside have become the same thing. Richard seems to be speaking, not to a crowd, as he would be in the theatre, but to a single bystander out of hearing of the other characters, to an accomplice. It would be interesting to know whether the actor visualized someone like that.

Compared to the stage, the cinema screen can provide not only greater intimacy but greater amplitude. Battles can be shown as well as talked about, and if there is any great cinema in the Olivier films it would be Agincourt and Bosworth. In both cases it is the work of the director, not Shakespeare, we are likely to remember. At Agincourt it is the charge of the French knights, owing something no doubt to the charge of the Teutonic knights in Eisenstein's *Alexander Nevsky*, but an unforgettable sequence in its own right. The angle of vision is everything, sideways on in steadily accelerating tracking shot with the line of horsemen stretching away in depth. This is intercut with the English bowmen, in stolid, immobile counterpoint, holding their fire. Soundtrack rises to a crescendo of drumming hoofbeats, finally to the whiplash hiss of arrows as they bring the charge to a halt. Horseopera? Well, yes, I suppose so, but also an extension into action of what the play says about the two armies and therefore epic. Bosworth, by contrast, is deliberately anti-heroic, a sodden, featureless bit of Midland countryside, where the sun can't be seen for mist and Richard, the doomed usurper, no longer believes his own pep-talk but rattles it off as if his mind was on something else. What it is to be dismounted, in Richard's situation, in country without cover, not knowing who will be the next to join the enemy – something like that is the key to the sequence. 'My kingdom for a horse!' in the text was never so meaningful before. But the ending needs more than a squalid realism, so film technique intervenes in the celebrated crane shot, looking down on Richard encircled by his killers and lunging out against them spasmodically *after* death. An angle, a detached visual pattern, suddenly give him back his importance, when a minute before we were with him, limping about in the mud. The crane shot is an alienation effect.

To my mind *Richard III*, completed eleven years after *Henry V*, is the better film of the two. Though the camerawork offers nothing as devastating as the Agincourt charge, it is more assured, more concerned with following the contours of the action than with drawing attention to itself. Apart from the final crane shot, it is most striking in the scene where Richard looks steeply down on Buckingham from the throne before discarding him. As well as underlining the obvious point about who's now on top, the camera angle refers very subtly to an earlier occasion when

Buckingham was the one looking up. He was at the head of a crowd of citizens, organized to offer Richard the crown, and his subordinate status was a fiction between partners. Now it is real, a fact the camera drives home. I think the superiority of the later film comes from having greater confidence in the audience. Being a pioneer work *Henry V* betrays some anxiety. It all happened a long time ago, the dialogue is to be archaic, much of it in verse, and so on. Hence the film opens in a replica of the Globe Theatre with the actors hamming in a way one hardly thinks Shakespeare would have tolerated. Even in its own time the play was conventional, we learn, so don't be put off by its rhetoric and formal behaviour now. This awareness of convention is kept up all through by the heraldic, formalized background to Burgundy's plea for peace, beautifully delivered by Valentine Dyall. Heraldic vines are an ideal background to the intricate speech. But against the repetition of these devices it can be held that they clash with the medium, in the way cartoon films with realistic actors fail to cohere. Either the heraldry points forward to a new and exciting use of symbolism on film or it amounts to a slick medievalism which gets in the way. It certainly conforms to the theatrical approach adopted towards *Henry V* and it may be a subtle form of apology for something archaic. My opinion is that it was worth trying, once. In any case, it was not repeated in Olivier's other two Shakespeare films, and a good film epic like *El Cid* does very well without anything like it.

Of the three Olivier films, *Hamlet* is the odd one out: tragedy where the others are epic, black and white where they are in colour. The ruling idea–'Denmark's a prison'–and the exaggerated enclosure of the action in dark, vaulted corridors seemed arbitrary at the time, 1948. It seems less arbitrary, more typical of a prevailing climate with every year that passes. From the first there were obvious echoes of Eisenstein's *Ivan the Terrible* in the measured, shadowy progresses through windowless rooms. Now one recognizes the affinity with a post-war movement of which one masterpiece, *Huis-Clos* by Sartre, had appeared four years before. *Hamlet* itself gives a pointer to the attitude of mind. The answer to 'Denmark's a prison' is 'Then is the world one', and the assumption of compressionist masters from Kafka to Beckett is exactly that. But there is an overriding objection to interpreting *Hamlet* in such a way. It is that the only person in the play who sees Denmark as a prison is Hamlet himself. What the film does is to imprison the entire action and in the process to slow it down. The result is to restore by different means the bad old interruptions caused in Victorian days by unwieldy sets. And the new means of interruption is the camera, lugubriously probing the corridors like a wagon in the galleries of a mine. Furthermore, Olivier is unsuited by temperament to introspective roles. Did he, perhaps, build up the gloom around him to help the adjustment to Hamlet? If so, it would have been wiser to opt for Renaissance hustle and glitter, and darken his own part against that.

Generalization from the Olivier films is difficult, because his merit is to have tackled the plays as three different problems. Nevertheless, there are a few conclusions one can draw fairly confidently. First, a lot of the holding power comes from all-round, literate speaking of the text; and this is a theatrical quality based on actors experienced in playing Shakespeare 'live'. You can provide it simply by recording a stage performance on film, as the Comédie Française have done. Second, the imposition of a cinema style outside Shakespeare is most noticeable in *Hamlet*, and parallel to the original it tends to be naïvely illustrative. For example, Hamlet meditates suicide on the edge of a cliff, a pre-Raphaelite Ophelia drifts down-river in the foreground of Gertrude's voice reporting her death. There may be no reason, in theory, why the camera shouldn't reinforce what the verse is doing. In practice, where the verse is doing its job, lyrical, descriptive or whatever, any illustration seems to me redundant, unless, that is, it is frankly pop art like Disney's illustrations to the Pastoral Symphony in *Fantasia*. And this leads on to a significant fact about Olivier's films, that the best of them is a version of *Richard III*, the earliest and least mature of the three Shakespeare plays.

Really, of course, there are plenty of reasons why Shakespeare's best work should not lead to outstanding cinema. He uses heightened speech, a thing with hardly any place in film tradition. One of his guiding assumptions is that there will be little or no illustration, and some of his best writing arises from the need to work on our imagination by words alone. Where he writes epic, as in the histories, the cinema can use his narrative skill and the conflict of dynamic personalities on the move, that is until Shakespearian epic reaches the climax of *Antony and Cleopatra*. Then the cinema, bound by its production costs and the need to reach a mass audience, reverses Shakespeare's creative process and goes back to prose. I wouldn't myself object to a film equivalent of Rome melting in Tiber, the wide arch of the rang'd empire falling, et cetera, any more than I object to Rauschenberg's illustrations of Dante. On the contrary. But the facts of the medium's finance are against any matching up. The more it uses its flair for spectacle, the less chances it can afford to take with elaborate dialogue.

How far can the cinema bring out the epic quality of Shakespeare's history plays? As far, I suppose, as audiences can be induced to tolerate heroic verse. Yvor Winters has written that 'the epic is, among other things, a kind of primitive history'. That is a definition which could include Westerns and the film of the Odyssey, starring Kirk Douglas. It could include Shakespeare's sources for his Wars of the Roses cycle, but not the design he makes from them, which depends on a mature conception of stability won from anarchy, on an exalted idea of the responsibility of monarchy and the limits of power. The design would be nowhere without the poetry, and because they harmonize it with the cinema's flair for popular epic, I regard *Henry V*, *Richard III* and the Mankiewicz *Julius Caesar* as the best Shakespeare films.

The last of these, *Richard III*, came out as far back as 1955, a decade ago, and there have been no successors. Why? I suppose because the blockbuster epic, which is the cinema's answer to television, can no longer risk verse. A bid for world markets cannot put very much weight on any one language. Having evolved an acceptable idiom for epic Shakespeare, the cinema drops him, for reasons that are strictly industrial, not artistic. In theory he can still be filmed with the actors in track-suits against an austere background, but he still requires large casts and enough actors of the necessary quality will be very expensive. Leaving aside its pageantry and setting, *Richard III* rested heavily on twin star columns, Olivier and Richardson. So did the magnificent Russian *Othello* on its star actors. By an odd coincidence that too came out in 1955, coloured with a kind of Byzantine garishness in tune with the way much of *Othello* is written. Nobody has made a distinguished Shakespeare film since, and what we think of this *Richard III* and this *Othello* is likely to reveal our critical attitude to the whole subject.

My own view is that, other things being equal, the film that uses Shakespeare's words well must always be preferable. As Yutkevich is directing a Russian language version we are getting what amounts to a double substitute. For the stage, in the case of a masterpiece tailored for it, we have the screen; and for the diction we have a translation. At this distance from the original, Yutkevich nevertheless composes a film which finds a noble and savage visual idiom for the action of the play. He follows its contours, the ebb and flow of the passions, by means of a wonderful feeling for the scale of figures in a landscape. This was done many years later by Cacoyannis in *Elektra*. It is the cinema's idiom for tragedy, the use of the screen and its rhythms for the necessary gravity; when the same director has command of Shakespeare's language as well, the result should be stunning. But only rarely has the right man had control of the expensive means of production, only Olivier, so far, in a sequence of films. And though the cinema has done enough to show its potential, its record over sixty years is frustratingly capricious. What is its one undeniable advantage over the theatre? It can confer immortality on celluloid to Shakespearian actors. And how does it make use of this advantage? It hands on to posterity Gielgud, the great Hamlet of his time, as Clarence and Cassius.

Whereas the cinema's record in Shakespeare falls drastically below the medium's potential, television's has been enterprising and imaginative within its own meagre limits. I'm afraid that in spite of the success and good repute of its epic series, *An Age of Kings* and *The Spread of the Eagle*, television is mainly significant as a means of diffusion. More people have seen Shakespeare performed in this way than in any other. A hundred million were expected to see Christopher Plummer's Hamlet, and I'd rather see it on television than not at all. But precisely because television reaches so many more people than the theatre or the cinema, because it has in fact superseded them as a means of diffusing Shakespeare, we need to be absolutely clear about its deficiencies, which are ruthlessly exposed by heroic drama. They spring from two things: the smallness of the screen and the group, not crowd, unit which forms the audiences. The screen is almost incapable of pageantry, even in the hands of a virtuoso crowd director like Rudolph Cartier. Compare, for example, his *A Midsummer Night's Dream* with Reinhardt's cinema version, or compare *The Spread of the Eagle* with the Mankiewicz *Julius Caesar*. The small audience units are allergic to rhetoric. Modern politicians, let alone Renaissance orators, have to scale down their delivery to a suitable intimacy. This leads inevitably to naturalistic Shakespeare, which in practice encourages the Method approach, notable on the stage as well for its tendency to work against the verse rhythm, because the phrasing depends on the actor's inner feeling rather than the scoring of the text. An excessively withdrawn character can come across well in such conditions, as Robert Shaw's Leontes proved.

In general, though, a distortion of Shakespeare's intention is unavoidable. It is difficult to make clear to the audience what the author has meant unless his plays, like so many of Ibsen's, were conceived in a more or less domestic focus. In Shakespeare on television it's repeatedly obvious that, with such a focus in mind, he would have expressed himself in a different way. The danger resembles the one pointed out in the case of the visual arts by Professor Wind; that appreciation of the original will be hampered by mass circulation of crude reproductions.

The Screen and Shakespeare Studies

Shakespeare's plays were written to be used by live actors in the presence of a crowd. It follows that all screen versions of them are subject to the limitations of the screen. Neither the actors nor their audience can conform to the conditions which the author had in mind. Instead of the text there will be a script; instead of the actor in person, there will be his image in two dimensions. Any situation in which the substitute looks like gaining ground over the original would have a vital bearing on Shakespeare studies, but today the screen, the substitute, has not only gained ground on Shakespeare productions in the theatre. Apart from a minority, it has superseded them; and the scholars and critics who make it their business to assess the plays and Shakespeare's intentions have scarcely begun to be aware of the fact. Yet around them is building up the pressure of a public, including scholars of the future, which draws its assumptions about Shakespeare from what happens on the screen.

This public far outnumbers anything heard of in the history of the theatre. For the BBC's *An Age of Kings*, the serial version of the history plays, the average viewing audience was three million; for its successor, the Roman plays titled *The Spread of the Eagle*, four million. These figures do not include audiences in the USA and elsewhere. If we bear in mind that the series were viewed in many places where there was little competition from the professional theatre, and in most places none at all, it means that the producer-director of these television versions, Mr Peter Dews, is by a long way the most influential interpreter of Shakespeare in the English-speaking world. Granting the skill and freshness of Mr Dews's approach, it would be a pity if his versions were taken to be definitive. For one thing, most of the star roles were inevitably undercast. Frank Pettingall's Falstaff was a jaded stereotype and Paul Daneman's Richard III was later to be seen at the Old Vic, with little success. For another, the small television screen is notably ill-adapted to Roman mobs. It may well be the wrong medium, anyway, for epic drama, whether Shakespeare's or not. But audiences in Canada or Bradford are not likely to have such reservations, and so a drastically limited image of Shakespeare gains enormous circulation, infecting audiences in particular with television's allergy to lyricism and rhetoric, in fact to any form of heightened speech. There is plenty of intrigue and horse-opera left in the histories, plenty of conflict and passion in the Roman plays, it's true, when they are taken as prose. We still need to be on the alert, however, when this has been done to a great manipulator of words who is also a dramatist. We still need to estimate the loss. What the new mass audience most obviously represents to Shakespeare scholarship is a pressure of semi-literate opinion. In as much as it won't tolerate verbal artifice this is ill-informed opinion; and it is steadily mounting, conditioned in part by the notorious limitations of television as a medium for drama.

With television scraping the barrel for living scriptwriters, its recourse to Shakespeare is inevitable, quite apart from prestige reasons. We must learn to live with the results. Compared to the medium's routine output they are excellent; compared to a good stage production they are cramped and perfunctory, at their best perhaps when the camera can hold one character at a crisis of emotion or a group round a conference table. The first fits the groove of hysteria in close-up, a cliché of television plays. The second conforms to a familiar layout in discussion programmes. In many ways, you would think, the cinema screen is the better one for Shakespeare. And so it is. It has room for epic sweep, for the battle scenes you feel Shakespeare would have been the first to elaborate if he had had the means, not to mention big areas of colour. Also it has a slight but distinct tradition of verbal rhetoric: Laughton's delivery of the Gettysburg speech in *Ruggles of Red Gap*, Muni as Emile Zola, Carnovsky as Anatole France in the same film. The cinema audience is already more of a crowd, a target for rhetoric, than the family group watching television, and crowds are easily massed on the cinema screen. As the reactions of the screen crowd are predetermined, the two can never be synchronized, but the live audience sees a lot of people listening to a speaker and will join in. When epic breadth and formal rhetoric were combined on film with a popular actor, the result was very satisfactory Shakespeare. I mean Olivier's *Henry V*. The trouble is that Shakespeare on the cinema screen costs a great deal of money.

As soon as big money comes into the reckoning, students of Shakespeare find themselves up to the neck in showbiz at its most garish and capricious. You can no longer hope for statistics because 1944, the year of *Henry V*, is as remote as 1600 from the mind of any showman of the nineteen-sixties. Knowing that film to have been a breakthrough, you might expect half a dozen of Olivier's best roles to have been filmed in the twenty years between 1944 and Shakespeare's anniversary; instead of which there is only a splendid *Richard III* and, working against the grain of his temperament, *Hamlet*. A meticulously prepared version of *Macbeth* is still on the shelf. Similarly, you might expect a follow-up to Joseph L. Mankiewicz's very good *Julius Caesar* (1952). It came, all right, in 1963, as a rescue job by the same director on *Cleopatra*, using Shakespeare's sources but not his words and wasting a first-class heroic actor, Richard Burton. This too we must learn to live with, in the spirit of *Put Money in thy Purse*, a sardonic account by Micheal MacLiammoir of his part in Orson Welles's *Othello*. Usually the history of cinema Shakespeare has more to say about showbiz, in its most bizarre Hollywood form, than about the Bard himself, but the most unlikely places can offer valuable documentation. I remember going to a Bradford cinema to see a Holywood revue called *The Show of Shows* of 1929. Suddenly there was a grumble of gunfire,

a glimpse of smoky battlefield and then the face of John Barrymore, a handsome vulture in close-up as Richard of Gloucester.
He delivered the soliloquy about Richard's deformity from *Henry
VI, Part 3*, using the identical phrasing and intonation and
spitting consonants that you can hear in his recording on disc.
It was every bit as good as Olivier's delivery of the same passage,
with a notable difference in context. Barrymore's came between
turns by Ted Lewis and Rin-Tin-Tin.

His unlikely intrusion on *The Show of Shows* is a good example
for the double standard you can apply to Shakespeare on the
screen. Here was a fine interpretation going the round of fleapits
in an ephemeral revue, presumably with no other motive than to
cash in on the actor's name. Barrymore had been a top star of the
silent films. Every schoolgirl had swooned over his Don Juan;
every schoolboy had gloated over the scene where they cauterized
him after Ahab's leg was cut off in *The Sea Beast*, a silent version
of *Moby Dick*. From one point of view his Richard of Gloucester
fragment is a variety act in an early sound film, a hunk of ripe
melodrama linking the turns of a comic and a performing dog.
From another it is, or was, a valuable document in the history of
classical acting. For a few minutes those opposites, the needs of the
box office and the needs of scholarship, happened to come together.

Unless we think the plays can be improved on by media which
didn't even exist when they were written, the cinema's only firm
claim to importance in this field is as a storehouse of individual
performances. Olivier's voice on the sound track of *Henry V* is a
good deal less thrilling than it was at the Old Vic in 1937, his
screen image a poor substitute for the living actor. What wouldn't
we give, all the same, for a film of Irving or Garrick? If the cinema
had been invented two hundred years earlier it wouldn't, as I
have heard suggested, supersede the critic. Hazlitt on Kean
would still be worth reading, because he reports and transmits
the unrepeatable live performance, the public 'happening' as
distinct from the studio 'happening', fixed eternally by the
camera. What the screen preserves is everything except whatever
it is that keeps an audience quiet when a great actor comes in
sight. The screen, in fact, conveys as much of his art as he's

conscious of himself, plus any intuitive bits that can survive the flattening, the shrinking to an image in two dimensions. Having done so much, the screen becomes of great value to Shakespeare studies, because the plays offer more scope to the individual actor than we usually care to admit, and a dominating actor can influence the criticism of an entire generation. It is important to know as much as we can about him. Hence the frustration which goes along with laughs to be got from the cinema's handling of Shakespeare, from a medium which records for posterity Olivier's Hamlet instead of Gielgud's, Maurice Evans's Macbeth instead of Olivier's, and from a crop of obvious candidates, no Coriolanus at all. Some of the results have been so good that it's not much consolation to remember that this is showbiz, that posterity was rarely in anybody's mind.

Ironically enough the most determined efforts to pin down famous stage performers were made when the cinema was least able to deal with them, when it flickered hectically and had no sound. A collector's piece of around 1913 put Arthur Bourchier and Violet Vanbrugh in front of a static camera as the two Macbeths. Although this ought not to be regarded as a reliable record, the performances are distinctly hammy, more so, I imagine, than later versions would seem with the sound track silenced. The movies take over when Macbeth's attackers camouflage themselves as Birnam Wood. One soldier raises big laughs by getting separated from the main body and scuttling back to them, still holding his branch. The Benson company's *Richard III* of 1911 is also portentously hammy, without any escape into comic relief. On the whole one prefers the approach of the people who made a one-reel burlesque of *The Merchant of Venice*, one reel of *Othello* as an animated cartoon. There was little point in tackling Shakespeare seriously until the movies could speak.

After the first primitive period, half piously theatrical and half frivolous, there was a lull until the talkies came, and with them Douglas Fairbanks Senior and Mary Pickford in *The Taming of the Shrew* (1929). I escaped from an unusually dull day's cricket in Manchester to see this film, but all I remember of it is Fairbanks eating an apple in church with incomparable Elizabethan panache. The speech of that famous couple of silent days was never their strong point. During the thirties, however, there were a few carefully prepared battles between Shakespeare and the cinema, ending in stalemate. Although Barrymore's Mercutio and Edna May Oliver's Nurse would be worth seeing again, Leslie Howard's Romeo and Norma Shearer's Juliet for MGM never took fire. In England, Paul Czinner directed an *As You Like It*, built round the elfin charm of his wife Elizabeth Bergner. As her accent and speech rhythms work against Rosalind's lines, the film is mainly important for its accurate and civilized recording of the diction and acting styles of Henry Ainley, Leon Quartermaine and the young Olivier. The classic of the period is Reinhardt's *A Midsummer Night's Dream* (1936), a unique example of a top theatre director at work on Shakespeare with the full resources of Hollywood. Here the best sequences have more to do with Mendelssohn than Shakespeare. The music goes along with a mobile, gliding camera as they explore the woods. It is true cinema, in the same decade as early René Clair. But nobody except Ian Hunter (Theseus) has a clue about speaking the verse. The enduring successes are a matter of inspired casting. Instead of being a lyrical charmer, Mickey Rooney's Puck is raucously earthy, a corner-boy of the forest. James Cagney's Bottom, the best I have ever seen, never forgets his local status. He is a craftsman; he sets up a play as if he were setting up a loom. This is twice as funny as the customary rural oaf, twice as poetic when the weaver grows a donkey's head.

Showbiz is only partly assimilated in the three big films of the thirties. Reinhardt has a Hollywood co-director, William Dieterle; the woods are alive with anti-poetic voices. MGM's Juliet is married to one of the firm's senior executives, Rosalind is the wife of her director. In relation to Shakespeare, that is what I mean by caprice. You have to remember the great performances which never found a place on the screen. When the breakthrough came, the Olivier films, it was a by-product of war. It began with *Henry V*, not seen as the crown of an epic series as we take it now, nor as GCE fodder, but as propaganda, with audiences predisposed to swallow the rhetoric. Generals were actually urging their troops on in terms of sport. It was no time for distancing the King by having him make his first entrance holding a cricket bat. That happened sixteen years later at the Mermaid, in a different world. If *Henry V* arises from the war situation, so does Olivier's *Hamlet* of 1948. It has a morose, claustrophobic atmosphere, dulled by the heavy masonry and dark corridors of Elsinore. Like the much later Russian version, it reflects European compressionism. The three Olivier films are continually revived, and I only want to make three points about them here. First, their availability gives them a vast influence on interpretation, more than a stage version can exert. Second, they are examples of epic and compressionism, open and shut, the two main forms of modern drama. Third, they are the result of an artist, who is a top actor-director, having full control of the means of production. The last of them, *Richard III*, dates from 1955, since when nobody of comparable authority has had the same costly facilities.

From the point of view of Shakespeare studies, foreign versions, even at the high level of Yutkevich's *Othello* and Kurosawa's *Throne of Blood* (Macbeth), are limited because they discard the text. This applies to Kozintsev's spirited *Hamlet*, which also leaves out the avenger's best opportunity. Even the stodgy *Macbeth* of 1960, with Maurice Evans and Judith Anderson, is more relevant, because it preserves acting of varied styles, including three recent Hamlets in the same scene. But cinema versions depend once more on the industry's caprices and television's far more enterprising approach is lamed by the visual poverty of the medium. The crucial fact is that neither of these handicaps inhibits the screen as a trend-setter. How far, for example, did Rooney's Puck influence the playing of this part in the theatre? Tom Courtenay's Puck in a recent Old Vic production was on the same lines. There may have been no connection between them at all. On the other hand, ripples sent out from the film years ago or in revival may be active yet. Sooner or later it must be the business of scholarship to find an answer. Again, how far was the Royal Shakespeare's *Wars of the Roses* of 1964 sparked off by the success of *An Age of Kings* on television? And what was the significance of Brando's Antony in the film of *Julius Caesar*?

The last question at least is easily answered. Brando's Antony has conditioned the playing of this role in the theatre as well as on the screen for more than ten years.

As I see it, the bearing of all this on Shakespeare scholarship is twofold. First, the screen provides a valuable form of documentation, securely based here on the National Film Archive. In using it the researcher can expect surprises. Even the early primitive phase of the movies has a major contribution, that is, Hepworth's silent film of Forbes-Robertson's Hamlet of 1913. Few would have guessed that this actor, renowned for his intelligence and voice, had also a range of gestures as rhythmic and varied as those of Ruggiero Ruggieri. With slight allowances for the actor's old age and the medium's infancy, the Forbes-Robertson film is not only a document but an unforgettable experience. Of films aiming only at entertainment one hopes that two adaptations of Compton Mackenzie's *Carnival* have been preserved, for comparison of Matheson Lang and Sebastian Shaw in the last act of *Othello*.

In its other capacity, that of trend-setter, the screen is potentially a menace. It has given Shakespeare his biggest audience. Up to a point it can lead that audience, but it is a mass audience which demands concessions. How far concessions can go we have seen in the theatre, where the meditative, the lyrical, the aristocratic and even the royalist and Renaissance aspects of the plays are toned down, 'rethought' or disregarded on the grounds that we don't see life that way now, or more likely from cowardice, from lack of confidence in the plays themselves. The air of apology whenever they are put on today owes a good deal to moving pictures. 'This', we were told at the beginning of Olivier's *Hamlet*, 'is the story of a man who could not make up his mind.' That is the authentic, over-simplifying, demagogic, package-deal tone of mass communication, equally insulting to the audience and to Shakespeare. One of its tendencies has already been to invade the theatre with screen values, screen emphases and even, as in *Henry V in Battledress*, the screen itself. Ultimately, the only defence against it will be informed, responsible criticism, as much at home in the techniques of cinema and television as in Shakespeare's text.

Whose Contemporary?

In discussing Puck, Professor Kott in *Shakespeare our Contemporary* quotes the following lines from *A Midsummer Night's Dream*:

> *Their sense thus weak, lost with their fears thus strong,*
> *Made senseless things begin to do them wrong;*
> *For briars and thorns at their apparel catch.*

This, he adds, 'is the good-natured Robin Goodfellow chasing the worthy Master Quince's troupe which has not done anybody any harm'. He sees Puck as in part diabolic and this incident as more sinister than it has ever appeared to me, either in performance or reading. The lines are part of Puck's report to Oberon of the troupe's flight when they caught sight of Bottom crowned with an ass's head. Their exuberant tone and lilting rhythm are not of the kind which Shakespeare uses to frighten us, though they are well suited to accompany the slapstick incident of a troupe of clowns on the run. A few lines before, the suddenness of their alarm is insisted on and compared to the dispersal of birds at the firing of a gun. What happens to the troupe is familiar to anybody who has ever tried to hurry through undergrowth. Even in daylight and without haste, the bushes can get stuck to your clothes. Indeed Puck, rightly proud of his mobility, boasts of his speed 'thorough bush, thorough briar', and perhaps we are meant to compare the blundering flight of the rustics with him. It would be possible to overstress Puck's fieldcraft at the expense of his diabolism, but I don't think the devil in him does much harm to the rustics, probably far less than the court's low estimate of their acting ability.

Nor would I agree that Bottom is ashamed of sleeping with Titania and does not want to admit his dream. Many a time I have seen English actors of the part make it clear that his awakening is essentially comic. He can't fully believe what happened himself, and he knows that none of the mortals in the play will ever believe that it did. Bottom says just enough to remind the audience of a secret he shares only with them. To view Titania's court as a group of midnight hags, the play as a study of brutal eroticism worthy of Goya, is surely to tilt Shakespeare's balance the wrong way.

In a scholar with Professor Kott's evident love of the theatre and familiarity with Tudor sources, one must try to find a reason when insight is threatened by recurrent lapses of judgment. Not only does he persistently darken Shakespeare's picture; at times he contracts it. He finds the world in *Antony and Cleopatra* little. 'It is narrow', we learn, 'and everybody seems to be nearer.' Again, 'the heroes are restless, like big animals in a cage. The cage gets smaller and smaller, and they writhe more and more violently'. Prospero's island is seen as a prison. This is the imagery of claustrophobia, and of the dramatic form which has embodied it for a generation and more. It is a product of our world, not Shakespeare's, and it has been used to transmit their experiences by many survivors of totalitarian persecution. If Professor Kott had led a sheltered life he could still have learnt to impose this way of seeing things on Shakespeare by way of Olivier's *Hamlet* film, which he much admires, and of the Warsaw production of *Richard III* with its background of iron bars. Since he is an active Polish survivor of both the Nazi and the Stalinist tyrannies, we can respect his criticism as coming from the front line of the Resistance literary tradition. There light casts only the shadows of prison bars and violence alone expands the confinement of an existentialist hell. As he says, 'This hell, "behind closed doors" does not need any metaphysical aids.' But it is not Dante's hell, or Shakespeare's, least of all when we remember how ill-equipped Tudor theatres would be to show it.

Although it's easy to understand why a Resistance veteran can find nothing funny in a flight through thorny undergrowth in the dark, the projection of menacing qualities can go too far. Bottom translated need not be sinister. He can equally well remind us of Sancho Panza, his ass, and Shakespeare's contemporary, Cervantes. Similarly, when Helena asks Demetrius to regard her as his fawning dog, the metaphor inclines to masochism but is scarcely brutal. We happen to know, from Caroline Spurgeon's analysis of imagery in widely differing contexts, that Shakespeare just didn't like spaniels. Here and elsewhere, one suspects that Professor Kott's honourable bias towards the bitterness of the plays has led him off course. Inevitably, too, there are limits to what he can find in the texture and connotations of verse in a foreign language. Quoting a passage from *Antony and Cleopatra* he claims that it could open a tragedy by Racine, without seeming to notice that it contains the word 'dungy', no equivalent of which could conceivably have been uttered on stage at Versailles.

Coming as he does to the plays with first-hand experience of violence and a point of view more precisely historically conditioned than most, it is no surprise to find Professor Kott at his best where Shakespeare is at grips with anarchy, that is in the histories, *Macbeth* and the crowd scenes in *Coriolanus*. *King Lear* does not yield to his approach, not only because its structure places it far outside the enclosed world of Beckett, but because exclusive stress on its anarchy neglects the escape routes from nihilism provided by the personal qualities of Kent and Cordelia, not to mention the triumphant virtuosity of the language, which enables us to digest the horrors in the certainty that the dramatist himself has managed to do so. However, it is valuable for us to be reminded of the pitiless face which anarchy wears in the histories and in *Macbeth*, for us to view murder as an experience rather than a stage convention. My only regret is to find such authoritative analyses weakened time and again by echoes of Artaud, the shrill theoretician of undigested violence.

Why has *Shakespeare our Contemporary* been such a strong influence on recent productions? One obvious reason must be the effect of occupation and the Resistance experience on avant-

ARMSTRONG'S LAST GOODNIGHT
Glasgow Citizens' Theatre, 1964

THE LOWER DEPTHS
Royal Shakespeare Company, Arts Theatre, 1962

garde literature, especially in France. Another is that translated versions depend on the physical action of the plays, their poetry having been reduced mainly to what it can denote. From Professor Kott directors may borrow an interesting and vigorous attitude, not too dependent on the verbal texture of the plays, which is scarcely mentioned at any point in the book. In compensation he has exceptional grasp of the workings of the power game, its losers and winners, 'who's in, who's out'. Following Brecht, our guide knows how much the plays have to offer simply as narrative. In England his book has inspired a down-to-earth, conspicuously well narrated version of the histories in the Royal Shakespeare's *Wars of the Roses*, duly fitted out with a decor of iron bars. It was also a dominant influence on Peter Brook's *King Lear*. This was as theatrically exciting as any production can be which allows the structure to be undermined by weak acting of Edgar and Edmund. It has been condemned for infidelity to Shakespeare even by such a connoisseur of avant-garde attitudes as Susan Sontag in *Partisan Review*.

Pop Shakespeare

Even before the event it could be safely predicted that the National Theatre *Much Ado About Nothing* would be a resounding theatrical success. The director, Franco Zeffirelli, has a genius for visual effects of decor and grouping, which he harnesses to his ruling idea of any play he interprets. He is a Florentine, and the tradition of his city is one of intellectual toughness and precision. So any ruling idea he chooses to extract from a play will be clearly understood by both actors and public. The twin themes of his *Romeo and Juliet*, for example, are 'love and the total breakdown of understanding between two generations'. In that production he wisely concentrated on 'the poetry of the human relationships', because English is Mr Zeffirelli's second language and he can scarcely be expected to have much of an ear for the complex rhythms of the prose and verse. To offset this handicap you might have expected the National Theatre to assign him a collaborator for *Much Ado*, and so they have. It is Robert Graves, who last saw Shakespeare performed over forty years ago. From this it must follow that Professor Graves's job is not to help the director and the actors so much as the public.

Where Zeffirelli helps the public by using superlative theatrical skills to put across his ruling idea of the play, Graves had made around three hundred emendations of the text, with the aim of clarifying obscurities. One of them concerns a few words which are quoted with admiration by Middleton Murry for the 'vast and homely perspectives' they open up, where Benedick says he found Claudio 'as melancholy as a lodge in a warren'. Presumably to avoid the modern connotation of rabbits, this is changed at the National Theatre to 'as melancholy as a ruined lodge in a deer park'. That's certainly less compact, and why does the lodge have to be ruined?

Again 'now will he creep into sedges' becomes 'now will he creep into the lakeside sedge', just in case a word in the *Pocket Oxford Dictionary* might throw us, although the sense would probably get through to any schoolboy who has fished for minnows. The play, of course, is noted for its rural English imagery; the villain sees himself as a canker in a hedge. I prefer the imagery undiluted. Another emendation makes one ponder on Graves's opinion that *Much Ado* is 'a popular comedy, not a literary play'. Where the original reads:

> *The practice of it lives in John the Bastard*
> *Whose spirits toil in frame of villainies.* (iv. i)

Graves had in mind:

> *The fault lies at the door of John the Bastard*
> *Whose soul delights in framing villainies.*

For a living process we get an inert, lying-down one, and instead of toil, we get enjoyment. For plural, organic spirits, we get abstract soul. In performance we were spared that rendering of the second line, but I scarcely need stress how easily the text could be emasculated if small adjustments became normal practice. On the other hand one might not quarrel too much with the motive underlying the Graves version, which is to clarify comic jargon incomprehensible to the audiences of today. What surprises me about the whole undertaking is its lack of confidence in the play and its deference to the audience, a deference not very far from contempt. You see, not all that long ago there were two successful revivals of *Much Ado*, one of them by Gielgud and the other by Douglas Seale, with Redgrave; and in neither of them was it found necessary to modernize the text.

What has happened since? The answer is Pop Shakespeare, that is Shakespeare packaged and marketed in such a way as to reach people living at our tempo, in our world, inhabiting our environment of supermarkets, advertisements and television. The energy and intelligence expended on the packaging have been prodigious. Good things were bound to come through. One of the pioneers was Guthrie, blowing up a few lines in *All's Well that Ends Well* to a desert army sequence of the Second World War. Later it was the turn of the First World War at the Mermaid, with silent film projections, the troops singing 'Roses of Picardy' and a real gun fired off. That was *Henry V*. With so many people growing up in the aftermath of war, hearing so much about it on all media, curious about it, yet without war experience, there was a boom in the history plays. The trouble with them is the way they lead up to *Henry V*, from today's point of view a sanctimonious aggressor whose first act as king was to disown his mates. That a Tudor audience thirsting for a stable monarchy would regard his act as reassuring and necessary, does not make it acceptable in Pop Shakespeare now. Hence Henry's reduction to an anti-hero as Prince and King. Planchon made him astute and cowardly, Littlewood a creep, the Mermaid an Ivor Novello hero in cricket flannels. In *The Wars of the Roses* he was cunning and uncertain.

Besides the histories, other plays in the canon have been distorted more or less into line with popular taste, enough at any rate to conform to the trends of pulp literature and mass-media drama. We have had the Shakespeare of youth, starting with O'Toole's first angrily impulsive Hamlet, going on to John Stride's pathetic Romeo who never grew up and leading to Albertazzi's Hamlet, a victim of night fears recovering on Gertrude's breast from the fright aroused by the ghost. Their counterparts in the comedies have been a string of scampering court ladies, like the twittering younger daughters in Hollywood period films. True, there's a lot of obsolete etiquette and verbalizing in the comedies, but this way the dust is blown off the classics and anyone can join in. The youth cult may even apply to *King Lear*. Why not consider the matter more closely from Regan and Goneril's point of view? After all, they are young enough to be his daughters. As well as reminding us how difficult Lear must have been to live with, Peter Brook's production illustrates the Shakespeare of Cruelty, though it must be rated a deviation from Artaud's doctrine, because that rejects not only the classics but intelligible words. Something can at least be done about the two consolatory passages which cushion the blinding of Gloucester and the play's grim finish. So it was that, in this production, the exchange of disapproving dialogue between Second and Third Servants after Gloucester's blinding was cut. And from Charles Marowitz's account of the rehearsal period we learn how the danger of a cathartic finish was overcome. As to the *Wars of the Roses* cycle, sufficiently cruel in the originals, Professor Kenneth Muir has remarked on the 'additional touches of cruelty' contributed by the Royal Shakespeare's adapter. All the foregoing distortions of Shakespeare, that is the devaluation of an epic hero, the cult of youth in a modern manner and the removal of correctives to the impact of cruelty, all of them make perfect sense in terms of current trends in the popular arts.

They make sense in terms of show business and the known entertainment habits of a mass audience. The problem is, how far can Pop Shakespeare make sense as a valid interpretation? I think a quick way to resolve that is to summarize the assumptions behind the examples I have given. Perhaps the most common assumption is that the historical background of the plays is variable, mainly by dressing everybody in the costumes of another period and directing the actors in such a way as to stress the anachronistic associations arising, with or without a suitable tailoring of the text. Between the text and the performance, of course, a lot can be done to get rid of the original intention merely by visual action, without any adaptation or cutting of the lines. For instance, the duel between Prince Hal and Hotspur can become a treacherous ambush. Next, the social background can be varied, usually by tilting the balance of sympathy in favour of the realistic, underprivileged characters, but also by stressing the youth of the nobility rather than their aristocratic code and manners. Then, as I have indicated in the case of *Henry V*, the epic purpose is regarded as variable. This is taken to be justifiable in the case of *Julius Caesar* as well, where Lindsay Anderson considers that in the last third of the play, 'Shakespeare's slavish cribbing from Plutarch is mere padding'.

Along with several other directors, Mr Anderson also believes that the plays are variable according to the interpreter's notion of dramatic tension. At the Royal Court he therefore felt licensed to cut the nine very Shakespearian, introspective lines uttered by Brutus while the conspirators are being escorted from his front door to the orchard. This assumption, about varying the text in relation to a director's view of what constitutes tension, merges with another one, which is that external action has priority over the spoken word. Often the casting of key parts can tell us where that scale of priorities operates. One other assumption, with a bearing on most of the others, is that rhetoric is a blot on the plays and always ripe for the axe.

Now, it's evident that in terms of Shakespearian scholarship and criticism, not to mention literate stage productions, all these assumptions are invalid. They bear about as much relation to the original as Orlando in the Sicilian puppet theatres does to the hero of Ariosto's poem; or as landladies in a seaside postcard do to landladies in Balzac or Dickens. Only, in Pop Shakespeare the packaging is glossier, the sales talk more sophisticated. Mr Anderson describes that Brutus passage he cut as 'rhetorical embroidery'. Sir Laurence Olivier looks for Dogberry, he has told us, in 'the mysterious impulse of stage logic'. How on earth is one to explain such a combination of arrogance and superficiality among gifted directors, claiming to interpret Shakespeare when what they are actually doing is adapting him to meet a lowest common denominator of admass culture? I think the explanation is that, in the age of telecommunications, Shakespeare in the theatre is a gamble. Crowds and heroic actors are expensive. The more you economize on décor, the more you must spend on the cast. What's mostly on the director's mind is not interpretation, but money, performers, and the public. Anecdotes about actor managers counting the house while on stage will remind us that these three problems are old ones. But now they have sharper teeth. In theory, the Royal Shakespeare and the National Theatre enjoy the conditions necessary for deep thought and careful preparation. Both, however, are newcomers on a continental pattern. In practice, they're still busy justifying their subsidies and chasing bigger ones. They advertise strenuously, adopt stances admired in the admass world, are committed to surviving in it at showbiz level. More urgent than a probe into Shakespeare's intentions is the search for a stage idiom that will be understood in Moscow and adapt readily to television. Into this atmosphere comes the director, often by virtue of his screen experience a connoisseur of pop values and probably one of their creators. He surrounds himself with performers equally aware of alternative employment waiting for them in three other media. He knows that the public they will act for will be predominantly screen trained, anti-classical, anti-aristocratic and anti-heroic, accustomed to packaging and gimmicks. He may have hit on a ruling idea which happens to by-pass the text, but keeps the reporters happy and offers a smooth passage to the public. Is he altogether to be blamed if his work reflects, not so much blank verse and the 'great chain of being' as all these showbiz factors inside and outside himself? One thing is certain, it will be easier to adapt Shakespeare to them, than them to him.

Having made more concessions to this jittery atmosphere than the plays can reasonably stand, the director has to justify them, not to the public or the popular press who have been met on their own terms, but to informed academic criticism, which always arrives too late to affect the box office. As he will not be taken seriously as an artist unless he can pass the scrutiny of this tribunal, the director defends his solecisms, anachronisms and distortions as best he can. Pointing out that there is no unanimity in the tribunal itself, he tends to claim that his ruling idea is valid, if not for the past at any rate now. Times change, as we know, and doctors disagree. We're all in this together, rethinking Shakespeare. Since the working environment I have described is a hectic one, and the plays show every sign of being well thought out in the first place, the claim to be rethinking them may strike one as over-ambitious. But the stock defence of free adaptation is that every period has its own view of Shakespeare. Sometimes this leads to questionable reasoning, as when Peter Hall tells us

that 'the political relevance of *Coriolanus* in France in the nineteenth century was quite different from what it would be now'.
Agreed, and so what? Why can't we project this most explicit of
plays as vigorously as possible, and let the current political
relevance look after itself? As a matter of fact, Mr Hall did
precisely that in his own excellent production at Stratford-on-
Avon. Yet this same director has recently said that 'the great
fallacy of the English dramatic critic, is thinking that you can just
do a play and let it speak for itself'. Well, he is a busy man who
deserves his fun. He can't really believe that any critic, English or
otherwise, thinks a play can be done without some advice to the
actors, and decisions being arrived at over this and that. The
truth is that some of us would like to see the advice and the
decisions inclined rather more towards the clues built into the
text, rather less towards the planned obsolescence of popular
taste. I myself, for example, prefer Mr Hall's own Roman
Coriolanus to the entertaining 'period' versions by Sir Tyrone
Guthrie and Michael Croft.

Because the staging of Shakespeare is so expensive today, the
director increasingly makes concessions to show business. As a
showman he is on safe ground; as an interpretater, he is driven
to rationalize what he has done by pseudo-critical explanations.
Of course every period has its own view of Shakespeare. That's
no excuse for disregarding the author's intentions, so far as they
can be discovered. Another favourite evasion is to stress that the
plays are only truly alive when they are acted. This can be used
to excuse vulgarization, provided it gets across. I think it springs
from an unnecessarily low opinion of theatre audiences. True,
we are square-eyed from viewing, attuned to the hipster's rhythm
of jump-cuts, close-ups and improvised gestures. But a thousand
or so of us in the theatre do not have to be stalked with the
equipment needed to hold fifteen million on television. The
perspective and the atmosphere of the theatre depend on what
living actors can conveniently imagine together, with a crowd
of people. Both need rest periods, or there will be no such thing
as a climax. Yet nothing is more widespread than the fallacy that
audiences must be offered instant comprehension. Market

BUCKINGHAM LIQUIDATED
William Squire in *The Wars of the Roses*

research has proved that they demand it from advertisements and television playlets. I've yet to hear of theatre audiences walking out on Brutus's Forum speech or abstruse Tudor comedy. Why, anyway, should we expect instant comprehension of Shakespeare, though not of *Ulysses* or Britten's *War Requiem*? Are we so much more moronic than those audiences of 1952 and 1958 who enjoyed *Much Ado* without Professor Graves's help?

Pop Shakespeare is based on what I believe to be a reactionary view of the public, that the mass audience is unwilling to exert itself or learn new things, needs everything spelt out. If one regards the plays as in any way valuable in their own right, apart from box office considerations, it marks a reversal of the revolution initiated at the start of the century by Poel and Granville-Barker. Today the work of those two pioneers would probably seem to us avuncular, cerebral and static. It would neglect the obsessive imagery and dionysiac emotion, shown to be latent in the text by Wilson Knight. But the Granville-Barker revolution was not dependent on changing insights and personalities. It aimed at, and achieved, high standards of interpretation based on deep study and respect for the text. And so it brought acted Shakespeare closer in line than ever before with the disciplines of literature, nearer perhaps to the stimulating conditions in which they were written. To reverse their approach is to impoverish both the theatre and literary studies, which are influenced more than is sometimes realized by the standards of performance. Does Pop Shakespeare also impoverish the public, while appearing to be on its side? Who cares, for example, if an anti-aristocratic version makes hay of characters derived from Castiglione? What have they to do with us? Well, according to Sir Leon Bagrit, the automation expert, quite a lot. 'Although the details may be different today from those of the sixteenth century', he writes, 'the fundamental concept is the same, that in order to be a full man you have to be a varied man. Your mind has to be adequately cultivated and your body has to be adequately developed and trained.'

That sent me back to those nine lines of Brutus so contemptuously cut out of the Royal Court *Julius Caesar* by Mr

Anderson. They certainly work theatrically. Visitors couldn't go from front to back of a big Roman palace in much less time, especially at night. Shakespeare uses the interval to build up suspense and remind us what sort of man Brutus is. Theatrically speaking, that doesn't seem too elaborate. Looked at as words in a play, the speech presents difficulties. We may not know who or what Erebus was, though the word is sinister. We may find it confusing that Brutus is addressing somebody called 'conspiracy', when no such person exists. Also there are three 'thous' a 'thee' and a 'wilt', which drastically need rethinking if we are not to be reminded what a museum piece the play is. On the other hand, the lines convey a direct picture of conspiratorial behaviour, rising naturally from the information about hooded visitors just given by Brutus's servant. There's the advice, 'hide it in smiles and affability', still daily followed in the rat race. Moreover, the speech refers beyond itself to the way the stage conspirators will behave when they arrive; and, for anyone capable of comparing one play with another, it closely anticipates *Hamlet* and *Macbeth*. By cutting this speech you are depriving the audience of an experience which some of them might want to make use of on the way to becoming 'adequately cultivated'. You are denying them the kind of enjoyment which Sir Leon Bagrit thinks quite appropriate to the age of automation. Whereas he believes in exercising the public's mind, Pop Shakespeare seems determined to empty it.

6. ON STAGE

West Side Romeo

A vaguely international approach is now the accepted way of staging the classics. At Stratford-on-Avon a young Pakistani actor was cast as Romeo, and Mr Franco Zeffirelli's version of the play was the Old Vic's outstanding success in a bad season. Briefly, International Style is an interim solution at a time when older actors brought up to favour the spoken word and young ones committed to inner feeling are almost impossible to blend in one production. Where there's no agreement in England or France on the broad lines of speaking heightened language in public, directors have found an idiom which conveys the dramatic action by other means. The dialogue serves as a commentary on physical action, groupings or personal feelings and the gist of it is all an audience needs to understand.

Clearly there are strong advantages in this way of going about it. You can use actors untrained in the classics to reach audiences unused to seeing them; you can tour the show untranslated. The reservoir of public ignorance about heroic drama is so great that you can sincerely call your work cultural pioneering. Casting no farther than two hundred miles from London, it's reported that Bradford, a city of 297,040 people, has seen no professional Shakespeare for the past decade. Many of the touring dates in the USA and Canada had never seen it at all. Wide open territory. The trouble is that all these places contain students of one kind or another, the meritocracy of the future, eggheads. These form a valuable potential audience, but I think they are too literate to put up for long with the linguistic weakness of International Style.

After a second visit to Zeffirelli's *Romeo and Juliet*, I am more than ever convinced that it is proletarian Pop Shakespeare, stylistically nineteen-fiftyish and dated as compared with, say, Hall and Barton's *Troilus and Cressida* (Stratford-on-Avon, 1960) or Croft and Hampton's *Richard II* (OUDS, 1960), both of which let dramatic speech do much of the work. From the standpoint of show business Zeffirelli's production, an expensive one by Old Vic standards, has paid off and has delighted young playgoers. Everyone agrees it has vitality and impact. But I think much of that is brought about through a by-passing of important elements in the script, and since the production is to remain in the repertory and go on tour, it is of some critical importance to gauge its weakness and strength. They are likely to condition the response of many people to *Romeo and Juliet* for a long time. The play badly needs rehabilitation, for several of the lines have become music-hall jokes and it must be twenty-five years since the heroine's part has been adequately done.

Here, at any rate, is an unusually precise confrontation of Shakespeare and a single interpreter, of director and text. We know that the director was in full control, that it was his first experience of staging Elizabethan drama in English, that his native language is Italian and that none of his cast is a top-flight Shakespearian actor. All credit, then, to Zeffirelli for his two successes: Friar Laurence, and, in the potion scene, Juliet. They come from two distinct acts of creative imagination, one considered and the other intuitive. Friar Laurence is simply given the authority and status a Roman Catholic priest has in Italy, and so, for once, is more than a subdued secondary actor. This means, among other things, that Juliet's fear that he has given her poison to drink, instead of a sleeping draught, is plausible. He is already a decisive, positive influence on the action. Judi Dench has our sympathy, as any actress must in this lonely scene of veering anxieties. But she is not left remote on the bed to convey them by words alone. Her misery sweeps her back and forth compulsively, seeming to fill the stage. Once she consults the audience, dumb, neutral observers. Every time she moves, a change of tone or subject in the verse is pointed. As the function of her long solo is to express inner feelings, the strong, sweeping movements and the sense of the words are enough. It doesn't matter that Miss Dench is not yet an authoritative speaker of verse. In this scene actress, director and set convey Juliet's terrible situation. It is an almost operatic set-piece, defined as such: 'My dismal scene I needs must act alone.' Zeffirelli uses the bed as a full stop. In the end Juliet returns to it, her refuge, and swallows the liquid as if she no longer cares whether it's poison or not.

I have never seen this episode done before with such tension and economy of means, the situation screwed so tight. I wonder, though, whether the effect of it would be much less if one didn't understand the language. On the other hand there are vast areas of this play which don't even begin to yield to a realistic approach. The balcony scene, for instance, reads as if Shakespeare was wholeheartedly intent on lyrical verse. Zeffirelli's insistence on compulsive movement all through it makes the unoriginal point that sexual attraction aspires to a clinch, and in doing so distracts attention from the verse. Worse still, it compels Romeo to stand with his back to us on a stringcourse half-way up the wall. Unfortunately one is inclined to remember this kind of plebeian scrambling later on, when the entire drift of the action invites us to take Romeo very seriously indeed, if not as an embryo Hamlet. More so when the shoddy naturalism of his poses forms a re-current motif, for in addition to attacking the balcony scene like a corner-boy scaling the wall of a girls' remand home, poor John Stride has to embrace the Nurse and to gambol round Friar Laurence. Juliet's entries and exits in the Capulet palace are habitually made at a run; and once she pirouettes several times.

The historical objection to this frolicsome youthfulness is familiar. Castiglione's Renaissance grandees never run; ladies are advised not to play wind instruments, presumably because it involves blowing the cheeks out like drunken Silenus. The dramatic objection has little to do with any antiquarian respect for social realism; it rests on the friction set up between kinds of behaviour and kinds of language when these arouse contrary associations in the minds of a theatre audience. Concede, if you like, that Capulet heads an Italian family in decline and bullies his daughter like a Tudor shopkeeper on the way up. That's still no excuse for emphasizing the effort involved in making an extravagant speech about Queen Mab. Either the conceits come easily to Mercutio or they don't come at all. By all means cut them altogether, but don't leave a quick-thinking actor like Alec McCowen to dredge them up laboriously, one by one, to an accompaniment of fatuous *ad libs.* from his friends. Dr Johnson insists that they are supposed to be gentlemen, Coleridge and Middleton Murry that Mercutio's lines have poetic value.

In fact there is scant evidence in this production that Zeffirelli has much interest in the poetry. 'I give thee *poison.* Thou hast sold me none,' says Hamlet–sorry, Romeo–to the apothecary, emphasizing the wrong word. Earlier he has turned to the audience pop-eyed, after saying: 'I had forgot that name', when the discarded Rosaline is mentioned. But after his banishment there is still time to raise Romeo a point or two above the family conflict and the misunderstanding between generations. His speech in the tomb scene over what he thinks is Juliet's dead body is of sustained gravity amounting to a stage direction. It moves slowly on a tide of open vowels. Part of its function is to distance the final suicides, ennoble them. No other analysis of the diction makes sense.

To understand what Zeffirelli makes of this final scene, we must go back to the beginning. Trained in neo-realism, a disciple of Visconti, he can locate a scene brilliantly, as he does during the prelude of *Cavalleria Rusticana* by assembling a crowd in the village square. He has done the same at the start of *Romeo and Juliet*, visually and by the emotive use of songs and church bell. It could not be better done, but in the case of *Romeo and Juliet*, although the impact is great, the relevance is marginal. So is the unforgettable inspiration of having Mercutio's friends take him at his word when he says he has only been scratched. In fact this idea misfires, because it gives his death the shocking surprise of an accident among children, whereas Renaissance violence was endemic.

SCOFIELD

Consistently enough, the last scene of *Romeo and Juliet* in this production is sentimental: two handsome young people untimely dead. They have been trapped, as Juliet was in the potion scene, and now they are given a final dignity by the lighting and the sombre bell. It is International Style at its best, a situation broadly and sensitively outlined. But Romeo's great speech has been delivered naturalistically. He is still the anonymous youth of the balcony scene; he has not been permitted to grow with the lines written for him or with the emotions gone through. Like Mercutio he has been cut down to the size of an adolescent in *West Side Story*.

A Case for the Carabinieri

While explaining his emendations to the original of *Much Ado About Nothing*, Professor Graves has been quoted as saying that he wouldn't think of amending the tragedies. The inference seems to be that Shakespeare's comedies are less valid than his tragedies, that adaptation of the comedies in the interests of present-day comprehension is more excusable, apart from the fact that there are jokes in the tragedies as well. I have three objections to this assumption. The first is that polished acting in comedy is a very severe discipline which has no room for short cuts, such as tampering with the text. Second, we know that Shakespeare's plays are related to one another in a continuous development, a fact we obscure if we respect one category more than another. My third objection to isolating the comedies, on any principle, is the way it encourages stock responses, for example that they are romantic, or dark, or in need of translation into modern English in case we no longer understand all the jokes.

A more rewarding approach is to remember that the audience is coming to see, not a director's grapple with tragedy or supposedly dated comedy, not a contribution to some critical theory or linguistic experiment, but a tested and viable play by a dramatist whose minor work is likely to carry the punch of his earlier and later masterpieces, at any rate in places. A man who has already written *Henry IV* and is later to reach *Hamlet* is not likely to need much apology for what comes in between, not to the extent of anxiety about our understanding of his more

ephemeral jokes. We know *The Merry Wives of Windsor* was
written to order, but *Much Ado* is another matter, and I think the
following points about its structure and motivation can be fully
substantiated. It has two plots, both of them leading to marriage. The first of them, that of Hero and Claudio, concerns an
immature, vulnerable couple. It is almost prevented by malice
and only saved by a stroke of luck. The second, that of Beatrice
and Benedick, rests on mature and predestined affinity and is
brought about by good-humoured artifice. No more is needed to
unite them, because the needling relationship they have fallen
into is an infallible proof of mutual attraction. They are both
outward-looking, exuberant realists, and finally we are to take
them seriously for the truth they have told about sex. Hence the
famous order to kill Claudio and its acceptance. Benedick acts
on it to the extent of making a choice. The structural basis lies
in the play-off of these two plots by continuous, implied comparison of the couples and the merging of two contours of action
when Benedick is ready to kill his friend. The triumph is to have
it all sorted out by semi-literate watchmen when aristocratic
intelligence has failed.

Motivation has often been regarded as a problem in the case
of the villain, Don John. I can't see why. He is a bastard, which
means that his way of life is entirely dependent on the good will
of his legitimate brother. Of Claudio he remarks, 'that young
start-up hath all the glory of my overthrow'. Like Iago's under-
estimated resentment of Cassio's promotion, Don John's loss of
some privilege or other is quite enough to account for evil conduct in an envious temperament. We don't require a full biography to accept what he does. All Shakespeare needs for his
purpose is a life-hater to conflict with the robust eroticism of the
others, a negative to set against the promoters of a marriage. Any
actor who can look morose and speak Don John's lines audibly
can supply an axis of evil for the whole play to turn on. A few
years ago at Stratford-on-Avon, Richard Johnson played the part
as a misogynist villain in the style of Lermontov, an interesting
variation. At the National Theatre, Don John became a snigger-
ing eccentric with a nervous spasm of the neck, in fact, blatantly

comic. When that is done to the villain, you can imagine what happens to the rest of the play. The nearest analogies I can think of to Mr Zeffirelli's production are modern burlesques of Victorian melodrama. A director who chooses to preface Hero's wedding by funny business with the collection bag is obviously not deeply concerned with interpreting *Much Ado*, and I don't intend to be drawn into solemn criticism of the result. For that, it may have been enough to summarize the qualities of the original, on which this colourful and amusing entertainment is based. What we're offered is farcical fantasy in a nineteenth-century Ruritanian Sicily, an evening which begins with a round of applause for a comic military band.

It would, in fact, be rather fun to seek textual justification for some of the things Zeffirelli has done. For example, Wilson Knight has emphasized the importance of the music and dancing to Shakespeare's intention. But I don't think this can be made to include the killing of two of Beatrice's best lines by music entries, before they have time to register, or the burlesque version of 'Sigh no more, ladies', which takes the singer's formal apologies for his voice too literally. Again, the conspiracy is discovered because Conrade and Borachio take shelter from the rain and are overheard talking about it. So I was quite happy to see umbrellas appear a short while before. But the mood of the production has to give Conrade a stammer as well, and to leave one umbrella in the sword hilt of a military statue in the piazza. If you want to send up a play by disguising the turning point of its plot, this is a good way to do it – this, and to set the stage by having an actor walk on to impersonate the statue. There's really no end to Mr Zeffirelli's inventiveness of irrelevant business, notably in the scene where Benedick is first led to believe that Beatrice loves him. Here three girls group themselves into the form of a baroque fountain and one of them suddenly shakes hands with Benedick before his exit. The effect is delightful if you are prepared to forget that this episode, far from requiring embellishment, is one of the finest in all English comedy and to stifle any memory you may happen to have of Gielgud acting it. Also, just once, there's something to be said for giving Dogberry's defective

English to a Sicilian carabiniere. Frank Finlay is excellent in the part.

All in all, this is an eminently exportable International Style production with the text interpreted like the script of an operetta. When the National Theatre possesses two houses, it will be able to balance this kind of entertainment with a straight English version of the original. In that event, I would suggest two changes in the cast. Maggie Smith is not the first Beatrice to appear unsuitably metropolitan and lazily voluptuous. A more likely candidate for the part would be Joan Plowright, a warm, outgoing personality who can yet seem detached. Benedick is a man with a hard centre, who ought never to seem anxious about making his points. Robert Stephens, with his rueful vulnerability, is too flexible for this, too responsive. For the logical casting of Benedick in this company we need look no further than Don Pedro, in the person of Albert Finney.

Deplorable Conduct in Cyprus

Othello is an actor's, not a director's play. It depends on the people who take the parts of Iago, Emilia, Desdemona and Othello himself. Each one of them at important phases of the action is left alone with the audience and the marvellous text. All actors have limitations of personality and emotional range, and when these are known beforehand, what they will make of the play can be fairly safely predicted.

The Stratford-on-Avon production of 1961, with Sir John Gielgud, is unique in my experience for drawing its cohesion from a performance which by normal standards can hardly be called Shakespearian at all. It throws away the verse. It disregards the dramatic points built in to the lines. The verbal orchestration might as well not be there. Take for instance the perky irony of 'Pleasure and action make the hours seem short', and consider it alongside the dark brown cello tone of 'Not poppy nor mandragora nor all the drowsy syrups of the world'. Here, they get the same treatment. Again, there's the tag, 'This is the night That either makes me or fordoes me quite'. This must be the first time on record an actor didn't belt it across. It is Iago we are talking about, of course, and he's not even military in bearing. One thing warrant officers have always known is how to keep still. They relax or they monumentally grow out of the ground, hoarding their energy. This one squirms and fidgets. Yet Ian Bannen's performance in its off-beat way is entirely successful. Mr Bannen is one of our outstanding actors of Puritans ridden by guilt. Vocally he lacks resonance and the legato required by heroic verse; facially he lacks dignity. This year he seems to have been exploring Shakespeare to find material apt for the Method notion of inner feeling. Here are some fascinating results of the search.

Iago is a Venetian guttersnipe, a slimy emanation of dark walls and cavernous rooms where no light comes, an infantile neurotic who latches on to Roderigo and Othello with an insinuating agility which nobody has time to question. He's hypersensitive. When he's reduced Desdemona to tears, he comes near to weeping himself. About to be tortured, he's too fascinated by the nearness of the corpses on the bed to be worried at all. No doubt the torture is a supreme thrill in store. The honesty everyone remarks on is emotional, unswerving loyalty to his own exhibitionism. Iago's cut off. Alone, he's unaware of the audience. In company he's never in touch with anyone at a human level, but he's always in touch with the emotional network between other people. He manipulates it. If Dr Leavis is right in thinking Iago essentially undistinguished, a mere precipitating factor of tragedy, then Mr Bannen's will do. It holds this production together, a pliable soft centre, as frail as the fatal handkerchief or the reflections we are given a sight of in the first scene, thrown by canal water on rotting walls. Dorothy Tutin's Desdemona, on the other hand, has a very firm outline, too hard for my taste. I think the play gains if Desdemona is voluptuous and passionate, like the one I saw at the San Carlo in Verdi's opera. She fought for her life like a tigress. Others have given a flavour of sex to the interviews with Cassio, a quite harmless touch of sensual insight aroused by her marriage. As it is, I find too great a contrast between Miss Tutin and the sultry Venetian splendours. The key to her performance is the obstinacy with which Desdemona presses for Cassio's reinstatement. So forthright a girl might have chosen Othello in protest against the colour-bar. But Miss Tutin is very good in the Willow Song episode, though what one feels is a mounting threat of physical danger, anxiety on her behalf, not pity.

Meanwhile, Franco Zeffirelli's magnificent, unwieldy sets have interrupted the momentum of the action again and again. But wherever the current is allowed to flow, it is through the main actors. The anachronistic realism which marred *Romeo and Juliet* affects only Brabantio, and in Iago it is a virtue. Bianca, it's true, is ridiculously burlesqued. But Mr Zeffirelli lets the main actors give us the play where only they can. For example, when the action crystallizes on Emilia, there is Dame Peggy Ashcroft at the top of her form. She knows what all this is about, verse, character, place in the crisis, all of it. For me this is the definitive Emilia.

Sir John Gielgud is not the definitive Othello. Who is? At any rate within living memory? Frederick Valk and Robeson were powerful, and utterly adrift from the verse. Abraham Sofaer had the music, the profile, but not enough more. Now Gielgud offers us a good deal of the part's orchestration, the first actor to do so for many years. And this he achieves while knowing–I've no doubt knowing quite well–that the explosive animality of many of the lines is far outside his range. I think it a great and courageous action for Gielgud to risk himself in the role. The Westernized gentleman Othello appears to be, that, of course Gielgud embodies with ease. The rhetoric becomes a normal mode of conversation, fluent and casual as the draperies in a Veronese; and incidentally it's worth a journey to Stratford to see how Gielgud manages a cloak. He lacks the barbaric kind of splendour and the animal magnetism that can ride the last act. His diction threads the climax mellifluously instead of dominating it. But Gielgud's plaintive bewilderment at any rate prevents Othello from sinking to a cornered animal or an old fool caught in a trap. These imperfections were inevitable. Against them are to be set triumphant renderings of Othello's address to the Senate, of his return to Cyprus, of Cassio's dismissal. I beg everyone with a regard for classical acting to see and hear what Gielgud makes of these passages. In them a great actor and some of the most fiendishly exacting verse in the English language shake hands.

Finally, Gielgud is not the tragic ideal of a military man. Zeffirelli's direction has provided for this in the long duologue with Iago which plants the jealousy. They play the scene naturalistically, two soldiers at work in the orderly room, signing

OLIVIER

orders and consulting files. Mr Bannen is obsequious, efficient, an army bureaucrat. Gielgud is genial, after the battle a grizzled commander tidying up. Love and marriage have been, for a time, dismissed. The irony of it! In the last act Gielgud conveys Othello's immense relief when he reaches for the weapon that is to end his own life. The weapon brings him back to something he really understands, his occupation. So Gielgud's Othello, by a subtle process of characterization, is military after all. In this role, however, to seem military from habit and experience is not enough. We need to be convinced that Othello is a soldier by instinct.

Scofield's Lear

For opposite reasons, Lear is as difficult to cast as Juliet. The actress young enough to look right for her earlier scenes can rarely project the suffering met with later. Lear, on the contrary, must seem old and still have the strength to carry Cordelia on at the finish, preferably in one arm, so as to leave the other free for gesture. By that time he is near the end of the most exacting role in English drama, one with a rhetorical climax written into the very first scene, where Cordelia is disinherited in an outburst like something out of Tamburlaine. No wonder we remember the play in terms of monolithic actors: Gielgud, Redgrave and Wolfit. This is frivolous of us, perhaps, though not more than going to hear the pianist in Beethoven's 'Emperor' rather than the orchestra. I like a touch of baroque excess in my Lears, on the lines of Michelangelo's Moses. The verse of the part does invite something of the kind, along with self-indulgent acting of a self-indulgent old man. Better still, I would like to see the mad scenes done with actors of equal authority playing Lear, the Fool and Edgar. These scenes are very modern and demand no less. They are expressionist, but the expressionist side of Peter Brook's production is not mainstream. Too much of it has been filtered through Artaud and Kott. One of the highlights shows Lear overturning a big dining table. But we already know that Mr Brook has a wonderful eye for theatrical effect. What else does it prove? Nothing new about the tragedy.

As always when *King Lear* is acted, his first scene gives many clues to the flavour of the production. It encapsulates the structure of Scofield's performance. The austere, clinical set and drab, leathery costumes admit no display of regality, so that Lear's later references to the court do not link with any ritual we have seen him take part in. But if Scofield is not allowed to be kingly, he still has immediate authority. The voice he adopts reminds me of the conversations in *Citizen Kane* between ruthless old tycoons. You hear it also in elderly generals, rasping and guttural; and in them it sometimes goes with a nimble physique, only to be recognized as senile because the movements are so abrupt. The physical apparatus of the despot is still in working order, but it has torpid rest periods and asserts itself intermittently. At the root of his trouble there appear erratic failures of judgment, such as Lear reveals in this scene. Where other actors have been content with formality leading to surprise and anger, Scofield charts the decay of a personality. The kingdom is being divided, 'that future strife may be . . . prevented . . . now'. He is not searching for the word 'prevented' in this most ironic line of all. The fractional pause before and after the word conveys effort, the insecurity of an old man's voice, however loud and penetrative.

When Cordelia opts out of the competitive flattery we are at the turning point. The usual course is for Lear to echo her 'Nothing' more or less incredulously, then to threaten her that nothing will come of this. Scofield does neither. He repeats the first 'nothing' tonelessly, like a reader testing for a misprint. Then he placidly invites her to speak again. He is now the patient teacher whose best pupil has made a slip of the tongue. The time lag in his comprehension enriches this episode and could be the prelude to his outburst. This never comes. Kent's intervention on behalf of Cordelia does not interrupt a dragon's wrath but an old man's impotent anger, which never rises with the resonance of open vowels in the verse. 'Call France!' is ordered in falsetto. Perhaps it's not anger so much as annoyance caused by surprise, old age's disarray at any disturbance of habit. The complaints are growled out with even more of a pumping effect after the shock has disturbed his breathing: 'Better thou hadst not been . . .

born . . . than not to have pleased me . . . *bettuh*.' We are gripped by a family quarrel; there is the threat of apoplexy in a board-room or over the port. Kent's banishment, a terrifying ritual in the feudal world and written with formal deliberation, comes across like the dismissal of a mutinous domestic servant. Curiously, and in spite of its avant-garde trappings, the produc-tion domesticates the play. Without properly rising to the trio and quartet of the mad scenes, it points up the Regan and Goneril plot. Never has the paring down of the ex-king's retinue been so brilliantly exploited, or the lines which define him as a hunting squire. Scofield's private residence is in Sussex, and outdoors his Lear's irritable growl put one in mind of the local rustic intonation. Is it Lear who overturns that table, or Squire Western, complete with riding boots and whip? Either way, if anything is to be made of his kingly office, it seems best not to see him too much from Regan and Goneril's point of view. Julian Hall's comparison of this performance to the Mayor of Caster-bridge is unflatteringly near to the mark.

As Scofield is a great actor, with all the equipment for a heroic protagonist of tragedy, including the virile declamation he let loose in *Venice Preserv'd*, I find it frustrating that the shape of this performance compels him to play down Lear's curses and to lack all conviction in the early appeals to his pagan gods. Wolfit was closer to the barbaric splendours of the part all through and Gielgud infinitely superior in the later stages, where the defeated are withdrawing into a remote, impregnable wisdom. Scofield does not, like the verse at times, aim to rival the storm. He greets it ecstatically as a refuge. His best moments are down-beat, when the old man's moods subside for a while and he comes to rest on a truth. Thus he builds a vocal climax on the last word of 'here's three on's are sophisticated' and holds a pause before adding, very low, 'Thou art the thing itself'. He reinforces this by the most intense scrutiny of Poor Tom, going as far as to kneel down beside him for a closer look. Another unforgettable thing is the musing, considered way he says of Cordelia, 'I did her wrong'. When he awakes in her care, Scofield's tone is level, subdued, and for the first time patrician. There is a glimpse of the royal, tragic hero who gets elbowed out of this rendering far too often, from fear of skirting Victorian portentousness, no doubt. As far back as Holinshed, Lear was described as 'a prince of right noble demeanor'.

Othello as Hipster

'Melodrama', whispered my companion during Olivier's Othello. It is indeed the portrait of a man with too little authority, dignity or worthy opposition to seem tragic in his fall. In execution it recalls the old days of actor managers, when the star is centred under a spotlight in a circle of artistic inferiors. In conception its outline is the impersonation of an elderly African, who listens placidly to the first of Iago's insinuations and says 'Why did I marry?' as if they were old friends gossiping outside a pub. At the root of the conception is Eliot's Othello 'endeavouring to escape reality', and pathetic in his self-dramatization. Only, Olivier is pathetic from the outset, abetted by a director who isolates him in a ring of senators. When the Venetian envoy asks whether this madman is the noble Moor he used to know, when Desdemona speaks of the grace and favour even in his frowns, it comes as a surprise, because nothing has been seen of such a person, nobody of whom Lodovico and Desdemona could speak in that way. Nor has the drab staging done anything to build up military status for him, though we know he can sort the guard out after a brawl. Cassio is unthinkable as a governor of Cyprus. As for Iago, viewed after Leavis as merely a catalyst, he's given no time to relish his cleverness or punctuate the workings of a schemer's mind. Thus reduced, he leaves us with the intended idea that nothing exceptional was needed to unhinge Othello.

Leaving tragedy, Machiavelli and Shakespeare's display of Othello's glamour out of the matter, why has Olivier chosen to suppress the Moor's heroic, stoical façade, which he could assume, if he felt like it, second to none? Well, the mood of the nineteen-sixties is anti-heroic, enough to enjoy the sight of Iago cutting the rhetorical warrior down to size. So Iago, with the authority of recent academic opinion, is weakened, and something other than rhetorical military appeal is needed for Othello. Hence the African impersonation, around which our feelings about racialism and our daily contact with immigrants can be relied on to crystallize, like Victorian sentiment round Irving's veteran of Waterloo. If the performance went no further than this inspired mimicry it would be no more than a tour-de-force, but we have to reckon with Olivier's unique combination of extravert energy and command of verse. Having vulgarized Othello, not only by mimicry and a homely chuckle, but by languid waving of a rose and one crudely florid gesture of respect to the Duke, how is the actor to keep a hold on the part for four more acts? He can't show the progressive collapse of a façade, the usual solution. He can, however, if he has Olivier's intelligence and stamina, directly express the causes of the collapse, the inner disruptive forces. He can release the sequence of feelings in which ravings like 'Goats and monkeys!' make perfect sense. This is a complete surrender to the text's many invitations to primitivism; its great achievement is to keep the beauties of language afloat on a tide of emotion, instead of swamping them. There is, for instance, no formal distancing of set-pieces like the address to the senate or the farewell to arms. Othello is too busy reliving the episodes to enjoy his own eloquence, yet the diction remains fluent and exact.

The axis of interpretation is Othello's infatuation for Desdemona. When she enters the senate, he concentrates on her as if they were alone. In the same way his disembarkation in Cyprus is made to seem a private occasion, a reunion without public significance, just as Lodovico's arrival later becomes an unceremonious intrusion, and the account of his wooing was a bout of tender reminiscence. In the disembarkation scene he has to say:

> *I prattle out of fashion, and I dote*
> *In mine own comforts.*

These lines may be the clue, thrown back to condition Olivier's subdued playing of the part before they are spoken and ahead for a while afterwards, until the crack-up. Before the collapse he dotes, a domesticated hero at his best in the presence of Desdemona. It would not be the first time Olivier has drained out the splendour from a role in the interests of an ingenious psychological version. He did that for Lear, a pathetic wispy psychotic in the actor's equivalent of water-colour. The difference with Othello's madness is that it's more violent, less sympathetic and disjointedly expressionist by any reading of the text. By planting its sexual basis in an intimately realized impersonation rather than a statuesque hero, Olivier rises to the scenes of collapse instead of dropping down to them. Interestingly savage in themselves, though scarcely tragic, they are happening to an individual we have got to know, not to a symbol of glamour. The glamour of the performance is in its violence, in the sustained animalism of an African gone berserk. What lifts it above melodrama is the accurate psychology and, finally, a wonderful modulation in the last act. Here Othello relapses again and again into his infatuation of the earlier scenes. The two themes of the performance alternate hectically. Then they join, as he kills Desdemona in the course of a compulsive sexual encounter. Olivier conveys the impression of a child who has broken the toy he values most and refuses to believe it. Now Othello's occupation really has gone, and in this version it was never the Army; it was Desdemona.

Never can his conduct have been made more credible. By working from inside the character, Olivier resolves apparent inconsistencies in the play, at the price of dissolving its exhilarating epic and political elements. Verdi knew better. I don't think Shakespeare was aiming at showing us how a displaced African ticks. Rather he was reviving Antony, blunt speech and all, perhaps as a trial run for the victim of Cleopatra. Before his last act rehabilitation, it was enough to remember Marlowe and bring out a latent Tamburlaine in Othello. The play works excellently in the theatre with little more probing than that. Of the Othellos I have seen, Valk had more power than Olivier and needed only one final salaam, in the tensest of silences, to explain the apartness of his colour. In Robeson's the colour didn't need to be explained and it was dignified by nature. Sofaer looked the part; his was dazzling recitation by a limited actor. Gielgud's was predictably nowhere near to the passion, yet beautifully orchestrated like much of the text. It remains to account for the flavour of Olivier's Othello, for the supple emotionalism which has made it so popular, built as it sometimes is on the wreckage of a bracing, heroic play.

He is an actor unusually responsive to climates of history outside the theatre. Before the Second World War his Henry V anticipated the response aroused by Churchill's oratory. Olivier's post-war Hamlet caught a European mood of imprisonment and defeat. His Titus predicted an avant-garde vogue for cruelty. After Suez he became the new Thersites, Archie Rice. During the racial convulsions of the nineteen-sixties Othello, I suppose, was inevitable. The journalistic, opportunist aspect of his impersonation is only too obvious, but it does not account for the emotional idiom he has chosen. This has a number of affinities with Hip sensibility as described by Norman Mailer in *The White Negro*: 'There is a depth of desperation to the condition which enables one to remain in life only by enjoying death, but the reward is their knowledge that what is happening at each instant of the electric present is good or bad for them, good or bad for their cause, their love, their action, their need.' The Othello who greets Iago's suggestion for the murder by saying 'Good, good: the justice of it pleases; very good' can be made to seem very near to the kind of mercurial creature Mailer is describing. It may also be relevant that professional soldiers are listed in *The White Negro* among the types prone to be psychopathic.

7. MALICE DOMESTIC

Redbrick Luther

A medieval knight tells us the place and the time. Behind him at
the Royal Court is a sketchy background of tall pointed arches.
Above him hangs a statue of Christ on the cross, ponderous and
threatening. Next minute we're taking part in the profession of a
monk. He is on his knees with his back to us. Incense drifts into
the auditorium and no acting seems to be going on at all. Ritual
plants us in the meaningful part of Luther's environment as
nothing else could. Another ritual assembles the monks for confession across our line of sight. Brother Martin, the monk who
had his back to us, is now in profile, half-way to becoming one of
them. They confess trivial sins of omission, hardly worth a
confession at all in the world outside. They're like old soldiers
ready to take their punishment as part of the routine, at peace in
the discipline. But Martin is half-choked by a feeling of unique
wickedness he can't put into words. There is a gulf between the
ritual and this man's spiritual needs. He harbours energies not
to be contained by the cloister and its régime. For example,
during a reading from the scriptures in the refectory, he is the
only one who really listens.

Then Luther's father visits him on the occasion of his first
Mass. There's a duel between them. Among other things the
father represents worldly security, materialism and a point of
view which regards monasticism as a retreat from responsibility.
It is like the conflicts now caused by social mobility between
philistine fathers and intellectual sons. But it's pure Osborne,

subtle and sensitive. Bill Owen gives the crude father enough insight to account for his son's respect; while Albert Finney modulates from the bovine intensity of the earlier episodes. He seems to lose a stone or two in weight. All at once he is a silver birch instead of a rooted oak. Like a judo expert he absorbs his father's onslaught by yielding to it. Then, instead of throwing him, he watches the other's good intentions emerge and answers them with a limpid receptiveness. A wonderful scene, marred only by the Freudian solution so confusingly referred to. Next the business of indulgences, the issue on which Luther unwittingly blundered into world history. It's introduced in a vastly successful alienation effect. Peter Bull takes over the entire theatre and gives us a sales talk, half American evangelist, half Anglican passion, quietly talking down. Acting, direction and writing are welded in such a way that anyone unfamiliar with that fatal abuse of Papal authority is given the essence of it in terms of total theatre.

As far as I'm concerned that ends Osborne's *Luther* as important drama, coherent under the most exacting scrutiny one cares to apply. It accounts for four scenes out of twelve, a proportion most living authors would settle for. The remaining eight scenes, two-thirds of the play, continue to be acted by Finney and directed by Tony Richardson with complete authority. So we're free to concentrate on the writing. You can sum it up like this: from now on the historical Luther became a public figure and Osborne's Luther doesn't. I thought we'd heard the last of his spastic colon. But no, references to the jakes continue until they amount to a snigger. And nothing is done to convey the idea that quite half of the great reformer's armament was in his head. He continues to be an alimentary tractarian and an inspirational preacher, impossible to imagine with his nose in a book. It's as if his career were being seen through the eyes of his father. Sure enough, the play ends in an atmosphere of tired domesticity, in the stereotype of a famous old man happily married.

The place at which Osborne parts company with the wider implications of his subject can be pinned down. It is the confrontation of Luther and the Papal Legate, the first rumblings of a revolutionary avalanche. The historical Cajetan was a Dominican able to hold his own with Pico della Mirandola in disputation. Osborne's, in a streamlined performance by John Moffatt, is like an Oxbridge don remonstrating with a junior research fellow from the Black Country. He has the cardboard outline you find in comedy of manners. So has Charles Kay's fastidious Pope Leo X. From now on we are left with the idiom of the International Style, its oversimplifications, its accent on feeling, its neglect of the human mind as a source of conflict in the theatre. It's the first full-blown success in that style by an English playwright. But it reduces our sense of Luther's danger to flames projected on the backcloth. And when we recall the prelate in *Galileo* or the Pope in Montherlant's *Malatesta* we know that Martin Luther calls for opposition on a scale like theirs.

'All right,' you may say, 'Why shouldn't Osborne underline the weary decadence of Leo X and his legate? The Papacy *was* decadent. You've been offered a scene between authority in decline and revolt in the ascendant. Now you're complaining because you weren't given a medieval disputation.' No, not quite. What I might insist on in this case is characters who give the impression that they know what a disputation is, who give, not so much a sense of period as a sense of weighty issues. People of consequence. Luther's public life calls for dramatic construction in steel or marble, not plasticine. A frivolous attitude to Papal authority diminishes Luther by leaving him little to sharpen his teeth on. The tone, emotional and satirical by turns, is inadequate to what's going on – which is the collapse of the medieval world order, no less. If Luther's obsessions are the main theme, naturalistic treatment and a limiting title might have been a good idea. Depth psychology doesn't go well with epic form, or with the broad, episodic effects of International Style presentation.

This is to take Osborne rather more seriously than he – artistically speaking – has taken Luther. Osborne as a playwright is first a man of feeling, second a satirist and thirdly a moralist. As a moralist he may lack the rigorously trained intellect necessary to tackle an egghead of Luther's dimensions, and in this play it's difficult to isolate his principal themes. But if two-thirds is artistic failure, it is a gallant one. What heartens one is Osborne's logical progression in choice of subjects. From the minor rebellions against parents and wives, to the stubborn nonconformity of Holyoake in *A Subject of Scandal and Concern*, and now to the historical roots of protest. It's a responsible progress and, however imperfect, the progress of a European dramatist no longer of merely local, or even national, interest.

The Wages of Sex

One of the infallible signs of artistic failure I have come to recognize in the theatre is visual. You couldn't miss it even if you were wearing ear-plugs. The ingredients of it are often a man, a woman and a desk. The woman is standing downstage, more or less facing the audience. Her feet are planted sturdily apart and level with each other, her thumbs are hooked into the side pockets of her suit. Unless there is tense climax in the air and complete conviction in the actress's mind, this is not a position of strength and she may sway a little at the waist, the way people do when they're embarrassed rather than excited by the work in hand. Meanwhile, at the desk upstage of her, the man is going through agonies, quietly cracking up and more than likely rubbing his forehead with his hands. Why is he upstage of her? Because the play's chiefly about him. This long-delayed appearance of a woman we've been hearing a lot about doesn't mean that her role is on anything like an equality with the man's, and the more strongly you cast it the more difficult it will be for the actress to conceal the fact that she's there as a technical device. But perhaps the dialogue can save her? Not if it's the sort given to Sheila Allen in this situation at the Royal Court. 'Why can't you trust me? Please!' she has to say, and 'Oh Bill! What are we going to do?' And the man's no better off. 'I can't tell you what it's about,' he confesses, 'I can't grasp anything.'

This confrontation happens at the very end of *Inadmissible Evidence*. The man's immediate problem is how to give this woman, his mistress, three clear days of his time, at the cost of missing his daughter's birthday party. But if the mutual confusion and indecision revealed by the dialogue I have quoted is to mean anything, it needs a very strong support in the total action of the play, before and after. Short of that, it amounts to neither more nor less than the old Pinero boulevard twosome, consisting of a man we're supposed to be interested in and a woman we're supposed to be impressed by, both of them acting like mad.

Significant drama never ends on that particular histrionic tone, either visually or emotionally. So working back, with strong presumptive evidence of failure, what's been going on? Well, for the first of the two and a half preceding hours, the most bracing high-grade entertainment imaginable. First, a slice of expressionism, with Maitland, anti-hero, in the dock for indecency and emitting the current affairs clichés of modern man as his brain gives way. The Beckett influence is so well digested as not to be intrusive at all. Maitland is a solicitor, and from now on we are in his office, treated to long speeches like nothing else in the modern theatre, with Coward's feline malice allied to the rolling invective of Shaw. A solid Osborne managing clerk and the usual bovine Osborne women represent two different kinds of work, for, as Byron remarked: 'It is terrible work, this love, and undoes all a man's projects for good or glory.' Indeed, one memorable point made is the stamina drained from the modern executive by infidelities, whether he's stalling both wife and mistress on the telephone or seducing the telephonist in a draught from the office door.

Thanks to a performance of genius by Nicol Williamson, Maitland can be accepted as the dynamic centre of a comedy of manners. But Osborne the dramatist is basically a man of feeling, in Jimmy Porter, in Archie Rice, even in Martin Luther. And so is Maitland. Of love, he admits, 'I'm not equal to any of it, but I can't escape it.' Now this is getting dangerously near to the passive sensuality of Graham Greene's Scobie in *The Heart of the Matter*, and there is more than a hint of Greene when Maitland interviews three women clients. The counterpointing of Maitland's pity with their drab recital of sexual needs, imposed, refused or misinterpreted, is an inspired idea which doesn't help the play forward. Why not? Because, I think, we are convinced by now that Maitland's feelings all round are too easy on the trigger, in fact, sentimental. Meanwhile, the progress towards his crack-up includes an interview with a homosexual client and another with his seventeen-year-old daughter, both heavily expressionist after the breezy naturalism of earlier episodes in the office. In the theatre, as in painting and on the screen, expressionism can be a cover for emotional self-indulgence, a substitute for deciding what you want to say and rejecting irrelevancies. So much time and theatrical skill is being expended on the destruction of Maitland that, in spite of Mr Williamson, we begin to wonder whether he's worth it. He's wise to the hypocrisies and absurdities of our society, from police corruption to weekend motoring, good. He's frank and witty about his enterprising sex-life, better still. But what about the superior sensitivity that seems to be claimed for him? Is his pity really for others, the victims of the archaic laws he administers, or for himself? If it's for others, why hasn't he managed to do something, other than rail at hypocrisy and lay all these women by the age of thirty-nine? And why, aside from the sentimental theatrical effect, is everybody abandoning him? In real life there's always an unlimited supply of replacements, male and female, ready to put up with an arrogant and wayward boss. But a spreading smokescreen of psychosis obscures any answers that could have been given. What we never learn is the playwright's attitude to the man who is on stage for nearly three hours.

If you sum Maitland up as an object of scandal and concern, the scandal – at a small-time office level – is uniformly vigorous and witty. The concern is inflated and sentimental. After that stodgy confrontation with his mistress, Maitland picks up the telephone and brings down the curtain with a last line about – going home! As to the general outline of the action, moreover, there can be no argument at all. The man we have been spending all this time with is irreverent, witty and abundantly virile. For this he is punished by a prolonged hand-out of the wages of sin. How very provincial, how very puritanical; and in a bleak, philistine sort of way, how very English.

English Farce

The great difference between comedy and farce is in the consequences. At the end of a comedy someone or other who matters has been cut down to size; an imposter, perhaps has been exposed, a tyrant has been humiliated, some luscious provincial nitwit has been seduced, or a metropolitan sex-pot has dwindled into a wife. However amusing we may have found all this, we know at the back of our minds that something has happened to these people. Life has been at work on them. Hence the well-known serious element in comedy, the faint residue of thoughtful anxiety which the best of it leaves behind. Nobody is likely to feel anything similar after enjoying a farce, because comedy, being more or less at grips with life is about 'us'. Farce, on the contrary, is about 'them'. I think this remoteness of the personages in farce is what makes it so fiendishly difficult to write and perform. We're denied any concern for them as people, for they can't be held responsible for their actions. In fact, they're inferior and the only thing they *can* be held responsible for is not making us laugh. Whether they are types or eccentrics or author's puppets to build a climax, the audience doesn't believe in them but regards them as conscious performers. This, in turn, gives a key position to actors who can survive such an exacting test and often reduces the influence of the playwright. He takes another step back from reality and begins to compose in terms of the things a select group of actors can do. Then he will find the actors continually insisting on things that run counter to his sense of construction, to the inner logic of farce, and in disputes it is the actors who'll win every time.

That, anyway, is how it works out in traditional English farce, relying on a nucleus of familiar performers, like the inter-war Aldwych team and today's at the Whitehall. Although the Royal Court revival of *A Cuckoo in the Nest* is still great fun, I was aware time and again of a slackening where the original actors were expected to take over. The whole play turns on a bedroom scene, in which a genteel drip of a husband has to spend the night in the same country pub room as the sexy French wife of an MP. On his trail are his own wife and equally formidable mother-in-law. They can be expected to turn up any moment, and it's a tribute to Ben Travers's conduct of the episode that we're still surprised when they do. But it's in his interests not to be found in that bedroom, so he creeps down to sleep in the hall, and there he needs to explain himself when the landlady discovers him on her final rounds. He says to her 'I'm looking for a *melon*'. Funny, but unreal, something only an actor working for a laugh could say. Then, having been driven upstairs and settled himself on the floor, he's ordered to open the bedroom window, an act of heroism in such discomfort. Yet, after all the stress on how cold it is, he can still find time to enjoy himself for a moment or two by flicking the blind up and down. Like the line about the melon this illustrates the unreality of farce personages, though it can be true in the sense that it fits a particular actor who can make us laugh. Another inter-war farce about hotel escapades was *The Night of the Garter*. Sydney Howard, a comedian with a vast lugubrious head and expressive hands, played some sort of butler or senior hotel porter, and the action would stop for minutes at a time while he did things with a telephone. I suppose one reason why amateur productions of farce are always excruciating is that the original depended so much on virtuoso passages, built into the actor rather than the script.

Now in *A Cuckoo in the Nest* quite half of the holding power of the central bedroom scene must have depended on Ralph Lynn's elaborate dithering while he bedded down on the floor, and Yvonne Arnaud's ability to make anything at all sound 'provocative', a favourite word in the twenties. Apart from the loss of this dimension, which is irrecoverable anyway, Anthony Page's direction of the most recent revival is a model of the way farce ought to be done. He has, in fact, refined the play by making it more in period than the original. Ann Beach for example, tones down the Arnaud part until it has the distilled, amoral quality of a Scott Fitzgerald heroine. As for Nicol Williamson, he has been well ahead of O'Toole and Finney in recent work, and I can't imagine either of them competing with the sense of style he shows here, that is, style by the Gielgud definition of 'knowing what kind of play you are in'. As a great actor in the making, Mr Williamson is from one point of view not funny enough for a Ben Travers farce, and from another too good for it. Both imposing and vacuous, he is very careful only to hint at a lisp and to concentrate on the reactions of a man in terror of his wife. One critic thought his anxiety was hysterical and concludes that the principle of acting farce seriously is therefore questionable. I can't say I agree with the conclusion. Sustained hysteria would be out of place, not because it's serious but because hysteria is basically a play for sympathy. As such it threatens the necessary detachment of 'us' from 'them'. And the same goes for any kind of physical violence, which had better not have any of the usual consequences, least of all, death.

A comic clergyman appears briefly in *A Cuckoo in the Nest*. He is a reminder of the secure, Edwardian class structure of inter-war English farce. There was an astonishing incidence of comic clergymen, as in the stories of P. G. Wodehouse. The best pair I ever saw were in a play called *Yes and No*, in which Felix Aylmer entered in search of his newspaper, looked hard at the sofa where his curate was in a clinch with the heroine, entirely failed to register what he had seen, and bustled out. But the revival a short time ago of *See How They Run* which fills the stage with clerics, did not take on in London. The Whitehall theatre team caters for a public less sophisticated than that of Ben Travers. They would be unlikely to understand his line in *A Cuckoo in the Nest* about someone moaning at the bar. Nearer their mark is the reference in *Chase Me Comrade!* to a Jerry, born in Poland, for these farces are the pop art of canteens and seaside piers, with no inner logic at all. Brian Rix as a civil servant, informs us that someone has 'busted' his braces, and when he impersonates a naval officer he dances the hornpipe.

Where the Whitehall farces draw on the defunct English music-hall and are best seen from that point of view, those of Ben Travers derive from French boulevard work and Pinero. They're still very funny and tell us a lot about inter-war England, but I think Mr Travers wouldn't claim anything more than an honourable place in the second rank. If Wilde and Feydeau, Pinero and Coward at their best, are his superiors, it's because of their stylistic coherence, in language or construction or both. They keep 'us' rigidly apart from 'them' and make no concessions to the actors.

Albee

For the last ten years or so, American drama has been in a very bad way indeed. The centres of gravity for new writing have been London, where the English new wave drama still has a foothold, and Paris, the home of Ionesco and Beckett, the avant-garde. Meanwhile the New York theatre has undergone a disastrous division. On one side there's Broadway, given over more and more to commercial gambles, to the logic of real estate, until it has come to rely on playing successes from abroad to expense-account audiences. On the other, there's off-Broadway, which caters for a small coterie following. The trouble with in-group audiences is the intimacy of the pressure they exert on writers, their fondness for turning the drama inside out, their readiness to put up with 'happenings' and similar gimmicks of technique. So the American playwright's usual choice is between Broadway hackwork and coterie experiments, more talked and written about than seen. In these circumstances to capture the Broadway public with work of serious intentions is a very good thing for the dramatist who can bring it off. With *Who's Afraid of Virginia Woolf?* Edward Albee has bridged the gap, and he's the first considerable American writer to have done so since Tennessee Williams.

Albee's first play was *The Zoo Story*, written in 1958 and first produced neither on nor off Broadway but in Germany. All it owes to the French avant-garde is its use of closed personalities, its one-act length and an adaptation of brainwashing to private life. The idiom and the background are notably and confidently American. There are only two characters, so far apart socially that the only place they could meet would be Central Park. Jerry, the outcast, neurotic one, needles Peter, the respectable one, the square. Finally Jerry kills himself by running on to his own knife, held up by Peter in self-defence. They're no longer closed personalities. They have got through to one another at a primitive level, and it's a tribute to the writing that the unlikely end seems inevitable. All the same, I think the wrong man gets killed. Jerry is not a hipster, an active, hedonistic psychopath who would kill for the kicks. He is literally Beat, and by that much nearer to the passive square. They are not really polar opposites as I feel they should be; but the conflict is intense, not a matter of verbal distinctions as in Ionesco, but of words underlining a conflict of attitudes the quickest way. On a broader canvas in *The Death of Bessie Smith*, Albee has a neurotic nurse goading first a coloured orderly and then a white intern with the same subtle malevolence.

Albee has the gift of finding an explosive situation, like those of *The Zoo Story* and *The Death of Bessie Smith*, centred on the dying blues singer refused admission to a white hospital. Within the situation he selects conflicting characters, one of whom dominates in the earlier plays, dominates not by anything so crude as invective but by misapplied psychology, by getting under the conscious mind, as in brainwashing. Now what is it that gives *Who's Afraid of Virginia Woolf?* an edge on the other plays? Two things in particular, I think. First there are *two* dominating malicious talkers to needle each other. Second, the form for two-thirds of the way is traditional comedy of manners. And comedy is a very useful package for serious intentions in the public theatre. Also it acts as a corrective to the vein of life-hating sexual disgust which recurs in Albee's plays. For example, Jerry's morbid description of his landlady in *The Zoo Story* sets out his revulsion in detail, far more than is needed to offend the square. In *The Death of Bessie Smith* the hospital nurse's distorted sexuality makes a point about racialism, but remains the most powerful thing in the play.

Who's Afraid of Virginia Woolf? is about a young campus couple who get caught up in the domestic war of George and Martha, an ageing, childless couple who could be taken as quite well adjusted, in spite of letting off steam. Indeed, it would be the height of comic effrontery to leave George and Martha coolly on balance at the finish. And for nearly two acts the tensions are absorbed in supple, irresistible dialogue, as if Strindberg had developed a buoyant sense of humour. Then Martha, acted by Uta Hagen as a woman of magnificent resource and vitality, is lingeringly brought down. First she embarks on an affair with the younger man, and it's a failure because he's been drinking. Then George, in an Albee brainwashing, peels away her ruling fantasy, the son who never was. As a resilient creature of hard comedy, Martha is valid, but in defeat she puts me in mind of a Tennessee Williams victim like Blanche du Bois. This is nothing like late O'Neill. We're back in the world of domestic problem drama with a Freudian key. We're apt to go home arguing about Martha's father and how George's parents died. I prefer Mr Albee in his tough, comic mood, the mood of George when he brings his full contempt to bear on an opponent who has found nothing better to say in his own defence than the words: 'Up yours'.

8. GREEK TRAGEDY

Greek Tragedy

When there is a deep lack of confidence in the classical repertory among theatre people, they tend to rely more than usual on recently tested methods of pleasing the public. Hence in the Restoration period some curious importations, like Caliban's mate, and in Irving's time, actor managers hogging the limelight against pedantically antiquarian sets. The clean-up started by Poel and Granville-Barker lasted until the end of the Second World War, and in isolated pockets of resistance to show-business values, until the mid nineteen-fifties. Its effect was to offer a full, accurate Shakespeare text, backed up by any devices of staging which came in handy without disrupting the author's intentions, as far as they could be determined. Anyone lucky enough to have seen Olivier, Richardson and Gielgud twenty years ago, will remember that audiences had no difficulty at all in enjoying the results. Anyone who has seen three thousand people intent on the TNP's *Nicomède* at the Palais de Chaillot, will know that the direct approach used for Shakespeare in 1944 remains valid for Corneille in 1965. But in the present theatrical climate it is no longer valid for Shakespeare. For the time being we are paying him the greatest compliment we know, that of 'rethinking' him in our own terms. That is, we are dismantling the plays into components marked 'Beckett', 'Artaud', 'Brecht', 'museum piece', 'rhetoric', and so on. The markings in most cases are ours, not his, but they are a faithful selection of current fashions and stock-responses. From this kit we assemble our adaptations and hurl them at the public with every available means of publicity and stage technology. In Czechoslovakia, for example, a recent *Hamlet* exploited a double image obtained by mirrors.

Much of this belongs to the history of popular art, and of the avant-garde, rather than interpretation of classics. It signals an attempt by the theatre to allow for a change in the perceptions of the audience, brought about by viewing. Behind the cutting of meditative passages and the pointing up of violence, there lies a desire for instant results. Too much fidelity to the conventions of heroic drama cannot be risked, in case audiences stay away or walk out. The idea that vigorous young audiences might regard it as a challenge to be called on for an effort of historical imagination is too bold, altogether. Nor is it thought likely that they might actually enjoy archaic language as well used as Shakespeare's. Managements seem to envisage a captive mass audience, larded with bohemian misfits. It is, of course, unrealistic to do so at a time of hectic university expansion. As usual, showbiz projects on to society its own anxieties and limitations. Meanwhile tested masterpieces are diluted and jazzed up in various ways, actors are prevented from growing up in the shelter of them and the public is denied contact with the big uncompromising episodes of drama, like Hamlet's reasoning and Lear's rhetorical curses. They are also denied rest periods allowed for in the construction.

Writing off Shakespeare for the time being as a mine of adaptations, too difficult for respectful staging and unprotected by anything as imposing and precise as a musical score, one looks around for any sector in which live drama can be massed in sufficient strength to survive absorption by other media. For whatever reason, there are few, if any, major living dramatists doing work as good as that of the best visual artists or musicians. The best bet for the nineteen-sixties in English seems to be epic drama, on the lines of *Oh, What a Lovely War*, *Armstrong's Last Goodnight*, and *The Wars of the Roses*, in spite of the latter's emphasis on anti-heroics and melodrama in Shakespeare's histories. This form, however, is more suited to screen than to theatre finances owing to the large casts required; and unless he is a literary genius, the writer's part in it is easily usurped by others. Towards the end of 1964 two events made me wonder whether we ought not to look in another, and in the circumstances rather unlikely direction, for powerful and relevant drama: in fact, to Greek tragedy. These events occurred on the margins of theatrical activity. One was a markedly undercast season of Euripides at a fringe theatre; the other was the publication of an expanded doctorial thesis. Both were the work of young classics graduates, very much aware of our own times. Their combined fields of interest ranged from abstract expressionist painting to quantum physics; yet neither of them was in any doubt that Greek tragedy can get through to modern audiences or that the public urgently needs it.

As it happens, the history of Greek tragedy in the English public theatre is slimmer than one might have expected. One of its pioneers was Lillah McCarthy, and when she appeared at the Court Theatre in *The Bacchae*, directed by William Poel, neither of them had ever seen the tragedies performed. That was in 1908. In 1912, she was playing *Oedipus Rex* with Martin-Harvey at Covent Garden, where Reinhardt had installed a projecting stage and the actors swept on to it from the auditorium. Henry James, a latecomer embodying the more leisurely habits of Edwardian playgoing, once made an unrehearsed appearance on the boards, caught up in one of the mass entrances of Reinhardt's chorus. Apart from the running time – 6.30 to 11.30 – it all sounds very close to the shock tactics we welcome now. So does Lillah McCarthy's opinion that Greek drama was not for the lecture-room and the bookshelf. What happened, then, to give English production of the tragedies its daunting image of hammy declamation by elderly actors, encircled by a genteel chorus? To answer that, you probably need a wide experience of Oxbridge and country house 'dramatics' between the wars. Although Lillah McCarthy was sufficiently tough to rehearse in public on the steps of the Tate Gallery and to hold a New York audience of thirty thousand, the London commercial theatre had no use for this kind of thing and her memoirs record total absorption into the Establishment of the day. We now see it as a bloodless edifice, doomed by the course taken by history, still ready to shelter vigorous Edwardian survivors and to welcome younger, conformist artists of promise, but brittle, inhibited and naïvely reliant on the English public school ethos. It was a good period, perhaps the best ever, for native classics in the public theatre, but the Greeks were mainly confined to private staging for a restricted cross-section of the public. For a group still addicted to the literary cult of childhood, Freud's discoveries were a particular menace to self-esteem. You would not expect the enduring psychological validity of Greek myth to be stressed in such company, or Dionysian impulses to be welcomed where the social manner favoured a cool restraint. Our inter-war Greeks were inevitably seen as parsonical, headmasterly Englishmen. The chorus were like submissive yokels or disciplined student nurses. The flavour of the plays was Apollonian, not with a blazing, irresistible intellect, like Shaw's for example, in mind; it was nearer to that hallowed cliché of English classical taste, the effete Apollo Belvedere.

I think we need go no further, for an explanation of the dreary inter-war image of Greek tragedy, than its embodiment in Gilbert Murray's translations. 'Greek poetry' wrote T. S. Eliot, 'will never have the slightest vitalizing effect upon English poetry if it can only appear masquerading as a vulgar debasement of the eminently personal idiom of Swinburne. These are strong words to use against the most popular Hellenist of his time; but we must witness ere we die that those things are not otherwise than thus.' Eliot was commenting in 1918 on a production of Euripides he had seen from 'one of the cheaper seats' at the Holborn Empire. His tone in attacking Murray is that of a man who expects dogged resistance for some time to come, and so it proved. He had diagnosed correctly that Sybil Thorndike, as Medea, was 'struggling against the translator's verse'. One must assume, I suppose, that this same verse was pumped out for the next twenty years on college lawns and in public school halls, without a struggle. It's a depressing thought, and more than enough to account for apathy towards Greek tragedy, even among the privileged minority affected.

The gulf between these pallid inter-war revivals and our own

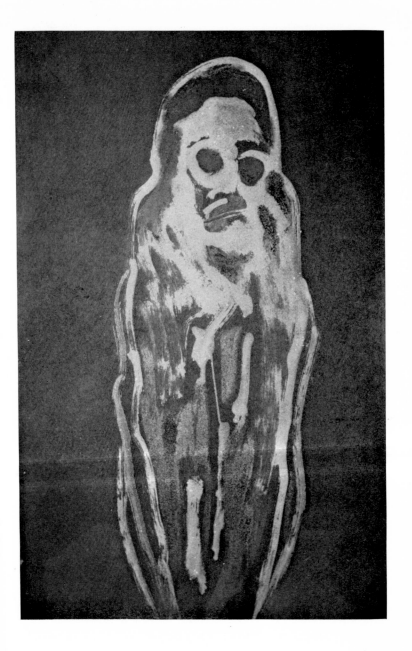

OEDIPUS
by Hilary Tyson, 1964

attitude to Greek drama in the nineteen-sixties is enormous, though the plays still have scarcely more than a foot in the door of the public theatre. Any initiative in this direction is inevitably an Oxbridge one, but 'theatricals' there no longer suggest the Edwardian ritual of an inhibited, self-deluding élite. Too many state-educated provincials have graduated in the classics, too many working-class plays have been put on by undergraduate societies. *The Times* reflected the brisk, impatient atmosphere by heading an article 'What's in Greek Drama for Us?'. And for the nineteen-sixties the short answer to that one would be Dionysus. In relevant additions to Mailer's tabulation of the hip and the square, Dionysus would take his place on the credit side, with 'romantic' as opposed to 'classic' with 'the body' as opposed to 'the mind', with 'to seduce by touch' as against 'to seduce by reasoned argument'. Whereas Apollo, at any rate in his inter-war role as an English gentleman in a chiton, would be irredeemably square. The reasons behind this preference for the instinctive, rather than the intellectual in the arts, are as complex as recent history. Applied to Greek tragedy, however, it is a preference likely to please theatre audiences, young ones especially.

Now, of the Attic writers, none gives the subterranean life of the instincts a better hearing than subversive, ambiguous Euripides, and nowhere more freely than in *The Bacchae*, with its mass hysteria and ritualistic frenzies. An English version of this play, directed with suitable energy, began going the amateur minority rounds from Oxford to the Tower, Canonbury, and finally to the Edinburgh Festival. Slowly but steadily it collected esteem and press notices on the way. It was the director of this production who, in 1964, mounted no less than three Euripides plays for eight weeks in repertory at, of all places, the Theatre Royal, Stratford. I say of all places, because this was the dockland theatre vacated by Joan Littlewood, a stronghold of native prole drama. In these unlikely surroundings Euripides drew an average audience of sixty-five per cent capacity in a four hundred and eighty-eight seat theatre over two whole months.

David Thompson's achievement was brought about without star actors and with none of the showbiz concessions usual in current Shakespeare productions. Clearly it indicates some demand for Greek tragedy, over and above the West End's very rare ventures in the form, invariably carried on the back of a star name like Olivier's. To account for the demand, I must briefly summarize a few recent trends in staging which seem to have helped. The four obvious problems involved are translation, chorus, heroic parts and décor, or more accurately, visuals. Most important of all, translations have moved away from the Swinburnian afflatus of Murray towards a flexible directness in a modern idiom. Many years of enterprising work on BBC sound radio have been a decisive influence, and how not to do it was shown in the National Theatre's prosaic and chatty version of *Philoctetes*. In most cases, though, a new flexibility has made the texts more viable for the theatre. Here is a random example of the change, from *The Trojan Women*, where Hecuba is addressing the body of a boy put to death by the victors. Murray's translation reads:

> *Ah, what a death hath found thee, little one!*
> *Hadst thou but fallen fighting, hadst thou known*
> *Strength, youth and love and all the majesty*
> *Of godlike kings, then had we spoken of thee*
> *As of one blessed . . . could in any wise*
> *These days know blessedness.*

In Neil Curry's version at the Theatre Royal, Stratford, this becomes:

> *Pitiful and unnecessary was your death,*
> *Poor child. If you had grown to be a man,*
> *You might have died fighting for your city,*
> *Having known the noble pride of youth,*
> *The joy of marriage and that royal power,*
> *Which makes a man a god. Your death might then*
> *Be said to have been happy—if happiness*
> *Exists in this grey world.*

To compare these is not to impugn Gilbert Murray's high merit as a classical scholar, so much as to underline how much better the later version is fitted for acting in the public theatre. Where Shakespeare, between the wars, needed injections of scholarship to rescue him from exhibitionist acting and got them from Granville-Barker, Greek tragedy needed bringing down to earth. The change has been a long time in coming, and the signs of it are most easily traced in the chorus. The refined, inaudible chorus noted by Eliot had 'contributed to the highbrow effect which is so depressing'. Sooner or later it had to go, otherwise audiences would be shut out of the action by what were supposed to be, among other things, their own mouthpieces on stage. The chorus still remains a problem, but recent solutions have had one thing in common. If it seems involved in the action, either by ritualistic gravity or mobile frenzy, the chorus can infect us with a sense of urgency and crisis. Provided this happens, the means adopted are a secondary matter. In Stravinsky's opera of *Oedipus Rex* Saint-Denis ranged them hieratically on flights of steps, remote and garish as the figures in a Byzantine mosaic. In Thompson's *Bacchae* they quivered erotically from head to foot. The Rondiris company had its chorus drilled to perfection in a series of eloquent gestures without loss of personality among the sultry, passionate actresses. With the advantage of filmed landscape, the women in Cacoyannis's *Elektra* looked as ageless as lizards or sunburned rocks. This flinty primitivism is one of the things we have a right to expect from Greek drama. From English actresses it's almost too much to expect, either from the pre-war genteel variety or the later, democratic, ones, sometimes victimized for going to a New Wave audition wearing a hat. Callas once said of her Medea, 'It's the Greek in me that speaks. Nothing to do with tragedy.'

Her Medea in Cherubini's opera was better, simply as acting, than any English female performance since the war. One of its sources was undoubtedly the American Method, and without the corrective of her Greek ancestry this would have been contrary to the mould of a heroic part. Twenty years ago, Olivier's Oedipus illustrated the usefulness of Shakespeare experience in a literate tradition. Brilliant younger actors like O'Toole and Finney lack this advantage. Owing to screen engagements, they rarely play the big parts more than once, and then under directors confused by avant-garde theory, social realism or the needs of other media, all of which are beside the point. There has also been regrettable wastage of one or two actresses made for tragedy, like Margaret Rawlings and Mary Morris. The solution is one which in England escapes live drama in general: to group the right people together where they can undistractedly get down to work on the artistic rather than the economic problems, in this case the raising of anti-heroic actors to big, heroic parts. Stars of grand opera are most of the way there already. A chorus is provided by convention and ritual by the discipline of the score. If the director of Greek tragedy in the straight theatre starts off with a good English version, he has our familiarity with opera on his side and operatic achievements to guide him. Then he is well on the way to solving three out of the four problems I have been discussing. They were text, chorus, and heroes. The fourth, if he's after dynamic visual effects, can be dealt with by reference to the ballet. Perhaps I need only cite Martha Graham.

We have the means, then, to revive these plays excitingly. Is the public ready for them? Leo Aylen, in *Greek Tragedy in the Modern World* has this to say: 'We are more constantly forced to think about death than our grandfathers were; but we have almost nothing concrete to help us to come to terms with the idea. One of the functions of tragedy is to help people come to terms with the thought of death. We have a great and obvious need to learn how to live with this thought, but no means of doing so. Tragedy might be the means of fulfilling this need.' This seems to me manifestly true. People bombarded by the horrors of war documentary, by nuclear terror, by sick humour, black farce and cruelty, need the ritual of basic drama, in which these things are put in their place and digested, not exploited. They are not going to get it from theatres committed to a philosophy of despair, to the fag-ends of romantic decadence, or a cult of sensationalism masking creative impotence. This is to whistle in the dark, and to sell audiences mean little prophylactic scraps of our mortality from under the counter.

Greek tragedy does better than that, without pulling any

punches. It could fill the vacuum created by the staging of our own classics without conviction. It has exposition built in, for illiterate audiences. Its subjects are violence, extremity, the human condition and remote authority. Psychology has given most of us a knowledge of its myths, and like no generation before we know its geography from the cinema and Mediterranean holidays. Whether we call what it offers us enlightenment or catharsis, Greek tragedy never cheats. But it invites the effort we think we do not need to make for Shakespeare. My favourite comment on it is that of Katina Paxinou. 'It is nowadays drama', she said.

Selected Bibliography

AVANT-GARDE

ANONYMOUS, 'The Theatre of Cruelty', *The Times*, 21st December 1961.

ARTAUD, ANTONIN, *Le Théâtre et son Double*, Gallimard, Paris, 1938. Trans. Mary Caroline Richards, *The Theatre and its Double*, Grove Press, New York, 1958; *Oeuvres Complètes*, Gallimard, Paris: vol. I, 1956; vols. II and III, 1961; vols. IV and V, 1964.

BARRAULT, JEAN-LOUIS, *Réflexions sur le Théâtre*, Vautrin, Paris, 1949. Trans. Bernard Wall, Rockliff, London, 1951.

BENTLEY, ERIC, *In Search of Theatre*, Knopf, New York, 1952; Dobson, London, 1954.

BROOK, PETER, 'In Search of a Hunger', *Encore*, No. 32, 1961; trans. in *Mondiales Premières*, No. 24, 1962.

DONNELLY, RICHARD C. *Criminal Law*, with Joseph Goldstein and Richard C. Schwarz, Free Press of Glencoe, New York, 1962.

ESSLIN, MARTIN, *The Theatre of the Absurd*, Garden City, Doubleday, New York, 1961; Eyre and Spottiswoode, London, 1962.

GIDE, ANDRÉ, *Les Caves du Vatican*, Gallimard, Paris, 1914. Trans. Dorothy Bussy, *The Vatican Swindle*, Knopf, New York, 1925.

GREENE, GRAHAM, *The Confidential Agent*, Heinemann, London, 1939.

14*

MALRAUX, ANDRÉ, *La Condition humaine*, Gallimard, Paris, 1933. Trans. Alastair MacDonald, *Storm in Shanghai*, Methuen, London, 1934; and as *Man's Estate*, Methuen, 1948, Penguin Books, 1961.

PRAZ, MARIO, *The Romantic Agony*, trans. Angus Davidson, O.U.P., 1933; Fontana Library, 1960.

COMPRESSIONISM

ALIGHIERI, DANTE, *Inferno*, Canto 33.

ANONYMOUS, 'Psychological Truth in Pinter Play', *The Times*, 3rd October 1961.

BECKETT, SAMUEL, *Fin de Partie*, Editions de Minuit, Paris, 1957; *Endgame*, Faber, London, 1958 and Grove Press, New York, 1958; *Happy Days*, Grove Press, New York, 1961 and Faber, London, 1962; *Oh, les Beaux Jours*, in *L'Avant-Scène*, June, 1964; *Play*, Faber, London, 1964.

BISHOP, MORRIS, *Petrarch and his World*, Indiana U.P., 1963; Chatto and Windus, London, 1964.

BLUMENTHAL, GERDA, *André Malraux, The Conquest of Dread*, Johns Hopkins Press, Baltimore, 1960.

BROWN, KENNETH H., *The Brig*. In *Tulane Drama Review*, vol. 8, No. 3, 1964; Methuen Playscript, London, 1966.

BURNEY, CHRISTOPHER, *Solitary Confinement*, Macmillan, London, 1952.

CAMUS, ALBERT, *La Chute*, Gallimard, Paris, 1956. Trans. Justin O'Brien, *The Fall*, Hamish Hamilton, London, 1957; Knopf, New York, 1957.

CHEKHOV, ANTON, *Uncle Vanya*. Trans. Elisaveta Fen, in *The Seagull and Other Plays*, Penguin Books, London, 1954, and in *Chekhov Plays*, Penguin Books, London, 1959.

FLEMING, IAN, *Goldfinger*, Cape, London, 1959; Pan Books, London, 1961.

GALSWORTHY, JOHN, *Justice*, Duckworth, London, 1910.

GOTH, MAJA, *Franz Kafka et les lettres françaises*, José Corti, Paris, 1945.

HEIMLER, EUGENE, 'Children of Auschwitz' in *Prison*, ed. G. Mikes, Routledge and Kegan Paul, London, 1963.

KITCHIN, LAURENCE, *Mid-Century Drama*, 2nd edition, Faber, London, 1962. 'Compressionism, The Drama of the Trapped', *New Hungarian Quarterly*, vol. No. 18, 1965.

KOESTLER, ARTHUR, *Darkness at Noon*, trans. Daphne Hardy, Cape, London, 1940.

MALRAUX, ANDRÉ, *Le Temps du Mépris*, Gallimard, Paris, 1935; trans. Haakaon M. Chevalier, *Days of Wrath*, Random House, New York, 1936; *Days of Contempt*, Gollancz, London, 1936.

MICHAUX, HENRI, *Epreuves, Exorcismes*, Gallimard, Paris, 1945.

O'NEILL, EUGENE, *The Hairy Ape*, Boni and Liveright, New York, 1922; Cape, London, 1923. *All God's Chillun Got Wings*, Boni and Liveright, New York, 1924; Cape, London, 1925. Both in *Three Plays*, Penguin Books, 1960.

PINTER, HAROLD, *The Birthday Party and Other Plays*, Methuen, London, 1960; *The Caretaker*, Methuen, London, 1960. *A Slight Ache and Other Plays* (includes *A Night Out*), Methuen, London, 1961.

SARTRE, JEAN-PAUL, *Huis-Clos*, Gallimard, Paris, 1945; Horizon Press, London, 1945. Trans. Stuart Gilbert, *In Camera*, Hamish Hamilton, London, 1946; and in *Three Modern Plays*, Penguin Books, London, 1958.

STRINDBERG, AUGUST, *The Father*. Trans. Elizabeth Sprigge, in *Twelve Plays*, Constable, London, 1963; trans. Peter Watts, in *Three Plays*, Penguin Books, London, 1958; ed. and trans. Valborg Anderson, Appleton-Century-Crofts, New York, 1964. *The Dance of Death*, in *Twelve Plays*, above.

EPIC

ARDEN, JOHN, *Serjeant Musgrave's Dance*, Methuen, London, 1960. *Ironhand* (adapted from *Goethe's Goetz von Berlichingen*), *Armstrong's Last Goodnight*, *Left-handed Liberty*, all Methuen, London, 1965.

BOWRA, C. M., *From Virgil to Milton*, Macmillan, London, 1945.

CHAMBERS, E. K., *The English Folk-play*, O.U.P., 1933.

ESSLIN, MARTIN, *Brecht: a Choice of Evils*, Eyre and Spottis-woode, London, 1959; subtitled, *The Man and His Work*, Garden City, Doubleday, New York, 1950.

GRANVILLE-BARKER, HARLEY, *Waste*, Sidgwick and Jackson, London, 1909; Brentano, New York, 1909.

ROSE, MARTIAL, ed. *The Wakefield Mystery Plays*, Evans, London, 1961.

REALISM

ARDEN, JOHN, *Live Like Pigs*, in *New English Dramatists III*, Penguin Books, London, 1961.

BEHAN, BRENDAN, *The Quare Fellow*, Methuen, London, 1956. *The Hostage*, Methuen, London, 1958.

GELB, ARTHUR AND BARBARA, *O'Neill*, Cape, London, 1962.

GORKI, MAXIM, *Lower Depths*, trans. Moura Budberg, Weidenfeld and Nicolson, London, 1959.

LUKACS, GEORG, 'Theatre and Environment', *T.L.S.*, 23rd April, 1964.

O'CASEY, SEAN, *Collected Plays*, Macmillan, London: vols. I and II, 1949; vols. III and IV, 1951.

O'NEILL, EUGENE, *The Iceman Cometh*, Random House, New York, 1946; Cape, London, 1947.

STANISLAVSKY, CONSTANTIN, *My Life in Art*, trans. J. J. Robbins, Bles, London, 1924.

SYNGE, JOHN MILLINGTON, *The Playboy of the Western World*, Maunsel, Dublin, 1907. In *Plays and Poems*, ed. T. R. Henn, Methuen, London, 1963, and in *Classical Irish Drama*, ed. W. A. Armstrong, Penguin Books, 1964.

WESKER, ARNOLD, *The Kitchen*, in *New English Dramatists II*, Penguin Books, London, 1960.

YEATS, W. B., *Plays and Controversies*, Macmillan, London, 1927.

SHAKESPEARE

ANONYMOUS, 'Shakespeare Cleared Up', *The Times*, 19th November 1964.

ANDERSON, LINDSAY, 'No Nonsense about Shakespeare', *The Times*, 15th December 1964.

BAGRIT, LEON, *The Age of Automation*, Weidenfeld and Nicolson, London, 1965.

CASTIGLIONE, BALDESSAR, *Il Libro del Cortegiano*, Venice, 1528. Trans. T. Hoby, *The Courtier*, 1561; Everyman's Library, Dent, London, 1928.

GRANVILLE-BARKER, HARLEY, *Prefaces to Shakespeare*, series 1-5, Sidgwick and Jackson, London, 1927-47; in 2 vols. Princeton U.P., 1946-7; in 4 vols. ed. M. St Clare Byrne, Batsford, London, 1963.

GRAVES, ROBERT, 'Making sound sense of Shakespeare', *Sunday Times*, 14th February 1964.

GUTHRIE, TYRONE, *A Life in the Theatre*, Hamish Hamilton, London, 1960.

HALL, PETER, 'Encounter with Peter Hall', *The Listener*, 19th November 1964.

KITCHIN, LAURENCE, *Mid-Century Drama*, Faber, London, 1960. 'Shakespeare in the Modern Theatre', in *Shakespeare: A Celebration*, ed. T. J. B. Spencer, Penguin Books, 1964.

KNIGHT, G. WILSON, *Principles of Shakespearian Production*, Faber, London, 1936; Penguin Books, London, 1949. Revised and enlarged as *Shakespearian Production*, Faber, London, 1964.

KOTT, JAN, *Shakespeare notre Contemporain*, trans. Anna Posner, Julliard, Paris, 1952; *Shakespeare our Contemporary*, trans. Boleslaw Taborski, Methuen, London, 1965.

LEAVIS, F. R., *The Common Pursuit*, Chatto and Windus, London, 1952; Penguin Books, London, 1962.

MACLIAMMOIR, MICHEAL, *Put Money in thy Purse*, Methuen, London, 1952.

MAILER, NORMAN, *Advertisements for Myself*, Putnam, New York, 1959; Deutsch, London, 1961; Corgi Books, London, 1963.

MAROWITZ, CHARLES, 'Lear Log', *Encore*, No. 41, 1963; *Tulane Drama Review*, Winter 1963.

MUIR, KENNETH, contribution to 'How can we improve Shakespeare?', *The Guardian*, 26th November 1964.

MURRY, JOHN MIDDLETON, *Shakespeare*, Cape, London, 1936.

OLIVIER, LAURENCE, 'Olivier on Choosing an Accent for Shakespeare's Peasants', *The Times*, 18th February 1965.

PURDOM, C. B., *Harley Granville-Barker*, Rockliff, London, 1955.

SPEAIGHT, ROBERT, *William Poel, and the Elizabethan Revival*, Heinemann, London, 1954.

SPURGEON, CAROLINE, F. E., *Shakespeare's Imagery, and what it tells us*, Cambridge U.P., 1935.

TREWIN, J. C., *Shakespeare on the English Stage*, 1900–1964, Barrie and Rockliff, London, 1964.

WILLIAMS, E. HARCOURT, *Four Years at the Old Vic*, Putnam, London, 1935.

WIND, EDGAR, *Art and Anarchy*, Faber, 1963.

MALICE DOMESTIC

ALBEE, EDWARD, *The Zoo Story*, with the *Sandbox* and *The Death of Bessie Smith*, Coward-McCann, New York, 1960; *The American Dream*, Coward-McCann, New York, 1961; all four, Cape, London, 1962. *Who's Afraid of Virginia Woolf?*, Atheneum, New York, 1962; Cape, London, 1964.

OSBORNE, JOHN, *Luther*, Faber, London, 1961. *Inadmissible Evidence*, Faber, London, 1965.

TRAVERS, BEN, *A Cuckoo in the Nest*, Bickers, London, 1938.

GREEK TRAGEDY

ANONYMOUS, 'What's in Greek Drama for Us?', *The Times*, 11th December 1961.

AYLEN. LEO, *Greek Tragedy in the Modern World*, Methuen, London, 1964.

CURRY, NEIL, Euripides's *The Trojan Women*, Newstage, London, 1964.

MCCARTHY, LILLAH, *Myself and My Friends*, Butterworth, London, 1933.

MURRAY, GILBERT, Euripides's *The Trojan Women*, Allen and Unwin, London, 1905; paperback, 1960 (twentieth impression).

Index

(a) List of Titles, all media; amplified in section (b)